Leaves from a Journal

The ball in the Galerie des Glaces, Versailles, August 25th, 1855

QUEEN VICTORIA
Leaves from a Journal

A Record of
THE VISIT OF THE EMPEROR
AND EMPRESS OF THE FRENCH
TO THE QUEEN
and of
THE VISIT OF THE QUEEN
AND H.R.H. THE PRINCE CONSORT
TO THE EMPEROR OF THE FRENCH
1855

With an introduction by
RAYMOND MORTIMER

FARRAR, STRAUS & CUDAHY
New York

Note

The publishers wish to express their gratitude to Her Majesty the Queen, by whose gracious permission *Leaves from a Journal* is published.

They also wish to thank Mr Robert Mackworth-Young, Librarian of Windsor Castle, for invaluable help and advice, and Miss Olwen Hedley and Miss A. H. Scott-Elliot, of the Royal Library, for their generous assistance in providing footnotes and helping to locate illustrations.

‑‑‑‑‑‑‑

Contents

List of Illustrations

LIST OF ILLUSTRATIONS

The illustrations facing the title page and pages 32, 48, 49, 80 and 97 are reproduced by gracious permission of Her Majesty the Queen; those facing pages 33, 81 and 96 by courtesy of the Gernsheim Collection. The likeness of Queen Victoria reproduced on the jacket is from a bust by Sir Francis Chantry, R.A.

Introduction

Whenever he talked about books with Queen Victoria, Disraeli addressed her as a literary colleague. 'We authors, Ma'am,' he would begin; for if he had written a number of novels, she had published in 1868 her *Leaves from a Journal of our Life in the Highlands*. In 1883 she produced a sequel to this, and was preparing a third volume when her wise and courageous chaplain, Randall Davidson, advised her in the most tactful terms against the project. Pained and angry, she asked him to withdraw what he had said. He could not change his opinion; and so he offered to resign his office. After a fortnight of stony silence, she sent for him and showed herself more friendly than ever before. The book never appeared. 'My belief', the future Archbishop wrote, 'is that she liked and trusted best those who occasionally incurred her wrath, provided she had reason to think their motives good.'

How characteristic of Queen Victoria! Highly excitable and impulsive as she was, in the end her sterling sense almost always prevailed. The episode also suggests that, like more professional authors, she thought well of her writings – and in this surely she was right. Her letters seem to me among the most enjoyable in English. Compared with those, for instance, of Lady Bessborough or of Mrs Carlyle, they are artless in the extreme; but the simplicity of her style reflects the shining simplicity of her character. She could not have dissembled, even if she had so wished – which she never did. Few letter-writers have revealed their feelings more openly. Her pen made everything personal and expressive, the phrasing, the changes from the third person to the first, the exclamation-marks, the indefatigable underlinings.

The number of letters she wrote – and in her own hand – is staggering. She also kept a detailed journal, sometimes written later from rough notes made day by day. Here she reveals herself from the first as uncommonly observant and gifted with a memory for the phrases of the persons who talked to her. The two books she published were made of extracts from this journal; and so was a volume 'printed for strictly private circulation' in 1880. Passages from this part of the journal were published by Sir Theodore Martin in the third volume of his *Life of the Prince Consort* (1877), and others by Mr Ivor Guest in his *Napoleon III in England* (1952). The book is here published as a whole for the first time.

Let me now remind readers of the background to the visits here described, and supplement its graphic story with details from other sources, including the Royal Archives at Windsor, which I received Her Majesty's gracious permission to consult and to quote. The Royal Librarian, Mr Robert Mackworth-Young, and his assistant, Miss Hedley, kindly helped me; and I am indebted also to Mr Roger Fulford for valuable advice.

In April 1855 Queen Victoria was aged thirty-five, and the happiest of marriages had already given her four sons and four daughters. She had not been born with a powerful intellect, and a lady-like education had neither strengthened her reasoning powers nor broadened her sympathies. But she was shrewd, industrious and possessed by an exceptional sense of duty. From her accession until her death she was to be in constant touch with the principal statesmen of her kingdom, who in those days were highly educated; and she knew how to profit from their wisdom: whatever they did, wrote or said was stored in her marvellous memory. She thus in time acquired remarkable knowledge and judgment, especially in the field of foreign politics.

When her first mentor, Melbourne, went out of office eighteen months after her marriage, she gradually became dependent for advice upon her husband to a degree unexpected in a character so resolute, not to say self-willed. To love for his person she now added ever-increasing admiration for his character and abilities. Soon he was taking his place beside her when she received her ministers, writing some of her letters and memoranda, determining all her decisions. When Lord Lansdowne and Lord John Russell returned to office in 1846, they were astonished to hear both the Queen and the Prince always saying 'we' – 'we think, or we wish to do so-and-so'. This account comes from Greville who continues:

> He is become so identified with her that they are one person, and as he likes and she dislikes business, it is obvious that while she has the title he is really discharging the functions of the Sovereign. He is King to all intents and purposes.

This report is confirmed by later statements of her own. In 1852 she went so far as to write: 'I am every day more convinced that *we women*, *if* we are to be good women, *feminine* and *amiable* and *domestic*, are not *fitted to reign.*' And six months after the Prince's death she told Clarendon 'she felt that her mind was strained to the utmost, that she was obliged to make decisions on her own, that she had never had to do so before, that it had all been done for her, that she could not bear it, and that she was afraid of going mad'. Passionate grief could not, however, enfeeble her sense of duty. Henceforward she kept a sternly attentive eye upon every detail of public business. Indeed, she spent so much time reading official papers, many of them trivial, that she had no strength left for showing herself to her subjects, and thus became for a number of years widely unpopular. This was one of her few grave errors, and came not from indolence but from a mistaken view of the relative importance of her various functions. We all know from her correspondence how strongly she felt about every sort of subject ranging from the wickedness of feminism and the narrow-mindedness of churchmen to the racial prejudice of the British in India. We need to remember that in 1855 when she wrote these journals she was content to adopt Prince Albert's views as if she had no mind of her own. The vehemence with which she expressed these views remained highly personal.

Our relations with France, friendly enough for the first thirty years after Waterloo, turned sour when King Louis-Philippe broke his promises in the matter of the Spanish marriages. We even feared a French invasion. His replacement by the Second Republic in 1848 did not restore confidence: the Queen and her Government had no liking for 'socialism'. Then Louis-Napoleon's *coup d'état* in 1851 shocked public opinion in Britain by its brutality; and his name in itself revived alarming memories. According to Clarendon, the Queen and Prince Albert 'laboured under the curious mistake that the F.O. is their peculiar department, and that they have a right to control, if not to direct, the foreign policy of England'. They detested Palmerston, who had been Foreign Secretary since 1846, and who, so far from accepting this view, repeatedly and incorrectly sent off important despatches before even submitting them to the Queen. Now he went too far: without a word to her or to the Prime Minister, he expressed his approval of the *coup d'état* to the French Ambassador in London. (This was Count Walewski, an illegitimate son of Napoleon the First, and therefore a first cousin of Louis Napoleon.) Palmerston had to resign, and was replaced by Lord Granville, a favourite at Windsor.

'With such a man as Louis-Napoleon', the Queen wrote in February, 1852, 'one can never for a moment feel safe.' Her general distrust of his character had just been sharpened by his confiscation of all the property in France belonging to the Orléans family, with whom she had resumed her friendship now that they had taken refuge in England. At the end of the year Louis Napoleon declared himself Emperor under the title Napoleon III; and needing an Empress he turned his eyes to Princess Adelaide von Hohenlohe-Langenburg, the daughter of the Queen's half-sister. Walewski was instructed to make feelers about this notion, which was ill received at Windsor, as was a later suggestion that his cousin Jérôme, best known as Plonplon, should marry Princess Mary of Cambridge (who became Duchess of Teck and mother of Queen Mary).

The vicissitudes of foreign policy, however, soon brought England and France together, each feeling its isolation to be perilous rather than splendid. The origins of the Crimean War are too intricate to be explained here, but four points perhaps deserve emphasis. First, Lord Aberdeen's Government was conspicuously pacific, and it is just such governments that usually land us in wars because our enemies presume that we shall not fight. Secondly, our commitments to defend Turkey against attack were vague, and such imprecision is similarly apt to land us in wars. Thirdly, Palmerston had chosen as Ambassador to

Turkey Lord Stratford de Redcliffe, who nursed a personal grudge against the Tsar, and whose desire for war against Russia made him neglect the instructions of his own Government. Fourthly and worst of all, public opinion in Britain was extravagantly bellicose, more so perhaps than ever before or since. The Russians, it must be said, had for long been swallowing neighbouring territories, and our imperialists feared further advances towards India. Our liberals detested Moscovite serfdom and despotism. Not content with cruelty to his Polish subjects, the Tsar had sent his troops into Hungary to suppress a revolution, thus earning here in 1848 the unpopularity incurred by Khrushchev for the same reason in 1956.

In June, 1853, a Russian army invaded and occupied the provinces of the Turkish Empire, then known as the Principalities (modern Roumania) on the pretext of protecting the Christian inhabitants; and the British Government now slowly and reluctantly drifted into war, because they lacked the courage to resist popular clamour. (These are Aberdeen's words, written repentantly before the war came to an end.) The Queen had perceived the disloyalty of Lord Stratford, and vainly requested his recall. The royal efforts to maintain peace became known to the public, probably through Palmerston; and at Christmas, 1853, just before we declared war, ribald broadsheets were in circulation attacking Prince Albert as a German who took his orders from the Tsar. Rumour declared that he, and even the Queen, had been imprisoned in the Tower as traitors.

Once the war had begun, it excited the Queen's enthusiastic support, and she became increasingly concerned for the neglected welfare of her troops. Her feelings towards Napoleon III, however, remained distrustful. In March, 1854, Clarendon, now Foreign Secretary, got into her bad books by advising that the Duke of Cambridge should accept an invitation to stay at the Tuileries. 'The Queen must and *will* protest, for she cannot mix up personal friendship with a political Alliance. The former is the result of the experience of years of mutual friendship, and cannot be carried by storm.' Clarendon answered, with apologies which barely veiled his annoyance, that she should never hear another word from him upon the subject of civilities to the Emperor.

[15]

Six months later Prince Albert, at the Emperor's invitation, visited him in his camp near Boulogne, and came back favourably impressed. The Emperor had been even more bowled over by the Prince – or so at least his ambassador in London was instructed to report. 'In all his experience he had never met with a person possessing such various and profound knowledge, or who communicated it with the same frankness. His Majesty added that he had never learned so much in a short time, and was grateful.' Laying on flattery with a trowel was henceforward the Emperor's technique.

The Queen continued cool; and plans for an Imperial visit to England were discussed but remained vague. Then in the following February Napoleon announced his intention of going to the Crimea and taking command of the campaign. This of course caused consternation at Windsor. 'It makes one tremble, for *his life* is of such immense importance,' the Queen declared. Besides, she could not endure the notion of her troops being placed under his orders. The Foreign Secretary should be sent over at once, she thought, to see the Emperor and discourage this odious project. Palmerston, who had now become Prime Minister, applauded her wisdom without revealing that he had already come to the same decision. Clarendon diplomatically suggested to Napoleon that he should wait until everything was ready for the *dernier coup de main*; and this was well received; but the plan remained a menace. The Queen and the Prince concluded that they must bring their personal influence to bear – and that is why they invited the Emperor and Empress to visit them during the following month at Windsor. Elaborate preparations were rapidly put in hand; new carpets and silks were bought for the suite to be occupied by the imperial couple; the furniture was regilded; the Waterloo Chamber was tactfully renamed.

To the Queen's graphic account printed here only a few additions are required. General Fleury, who came with Napoleon, tells us in his memoirs that the Empress's dress, admired by the Queen on the first evening, was borrowed from one of her ladies, because her luggage had not arrived. The notebook on which the journal was based includes a sketch by the Queen of a skirt worn by Eugénie, with the comment 'charming'. Lady Clarendon noted the voluminousness of the imperial skirts, which reminded her of old-time paniers: this must have been the first appearance in England of the crinoline. The manuscript at Windsor contains a few phrases omitted in the privately printed edition. Already on the third day of the visit the Queen refers to 'the dear, sweet Empress', who according to the Emperor 'naturally feels the *gêne* of her position from not having been brought up to it'. A letter during the visit from the Queen to Princess Augusta of Prussia includes one significant phrase about the Emperor, 'he has a great deal of German and nothing French in his character'. This of course was intended as praise: he skilfully exploited at Windsor the knowledge of Germany he had acquired as a student in Bavaria. (Like the Queen, he spoke French and English with a German accent.) To her uncle, King Leopold of Belgium, the Queen wrote: 'There is great fascination in the quiet manner of the Emperor, and *she* is very pleasing, very graceful, and very unaffected but very delicate. She *is* certainly very pretty and very uncommon-looking.'

This was a triumph over prejudice. When the Emperor announced his betrothal to Mlle de Montijo, the Queen had reported her to be 'beautiful, clever, very coquette, passionate and wild'. Prince Albert's brother Ernst believed her to be Palmerston's daughter, perhaps confusing him with Clarendon, who certainly had been her mother's fervent admirer. The Emperor soon after his marriage rushed up to his mother-in-law with a letter declaring Eugénie to be Clarendon's daughter. The answer came pat, 'Mais, sire, les dates ne correspondent pas'. During the royal visit to Paris Mme de Montijo repeated this story to Clarendon, who repeated it to his wife. The affair had ended long before her marriage, but she was not amused.

Ten days after the Windsor visit the Queen summed up her impressions in a memorandum too long for quotation here. It pays tribute to his great qualities, but 'how far he is actuated by a strong *moral* sense of *right* and *wrong* is difficult to say'. Still, she would 'rely with confidence on his behaving honestly and faithfully towards us', and 'I would go still further and think that it is in our power to *keep* him in the right course, and to protect him against the extreme flightiness, changeableness, and to a certain extent want of honesty of his own servants and nation'.

B

INTRODUCTION

The return visit of the Queen and Prince Albert, who took with them their two eldest children, demanded a new set of elaborate arrangements. Several points were happily cleared up by correspondence beforehand. Lord Cowley, the British Ambassador in Paris, sent a message from the Empress: she asked to be forgiven if she could not attend all the festivities, as she was due to bear a child in the early spring. The answer came: 'the Queen would be quite *miserable* if the Empress exerted herself on our account'. There was talk of cancelling a concert proposed for the first Sunday, because it might offend sabbatarian feeling in England (which the Queen never shared). A concert was given, however, on the second Sunday of the visit. Then there was the matter of precedence, the rules of which were not the same in France as in England. The Queen declared that the Emperor must be entirely free to follow his own wishes, as she considered herself to be in her own country. The trouble seems to have been that Prince Albert's rank was doubtful. Even when he was given the title of Prince Consort two years later, Austria remained obdurate, Metternich protesting that he could no more make a man royal who was not than he could make him eight feet high. Napoleon, however, was intent upon gratifying his guests, and gave the Prince all the status that could be desired. His old uncle Jérôme, the ex-King of Westphalia, refused to follow his example, and therefore absented himself from all the ceremonies, although he did pay a private call upon the Queen and her husband.

The royal train arrived in Paris late; the crowds were kept waiting for hours; it was then too dark to see the Queen properly; and she had not changed her straw travelling-bonnet for anything more elegant. Her reception therefore was a little frigid, which she seems not to have noticed. Her later appearances excited rapture, and we are told that 'her constant smile took the fancy of the people'. She had stayed twelve years previously with King Louis-Philippe at the Château d'Eu in Normandy, but had never been to the capital. Indeed, she was the first reigning English sovereign to visit Paris since 1431, when Henry VI was crowned King of France in Notre-Dame. Prince Albert had been there once as a boy of fifteen. The few letters she had time to write during the visit are just as

[18]

enthusiastic as the journal; 'I have formed a great affection for the Emperor . . . The dear and *very* charming Empress (whom Albert likes particularly) . . . I am *delighted, enchanted, amused* and *interested'*. The weather was extremely hot, and the Queen detested heat; yet she proved an indefatigable sightseer. At the Opera the contrast was conspicuous between her figure and that of the willowy Empress. The Parisians noticed, however, that when they sat down after the national anthems the *parvenue* Eugénie looked round to see that her chair was rightly placed, and the Queen did not: born royal she knew that it would be.

The manuscript journal at Windsor includes further references to the excellence of the serving at meals, 'much more royal and dignified' than in the previous reign, and to the bad manners of Prince Napoleon, 'very disagreeable, disagreeing with everybody and being thoroughly rude'. Also his sister, Princesse Mathilde, is described as 'no longer handsome, very stout and not distinguished looking'. (Clarendon amused the Maids of Honour by nicknaming this pair 'the assassin' and 'the cook'.) Before departing the Queen presented £1,000 to the poor of Paris, and £100 to the poor of Saint-Cloud, £1,500 to the servants, and jewels or snuff-boxes to the members of the Imperial Household, the *Préfet* and other dignitaries. The Embassy chaplain who had 'read prayers' on the two Sundays received a ring. The bill at Garrard's for these presents was £4,313.

Three days after her return the Queen sent to Stockmar a long letter brimming with enthusiasm:

> I never enjoyed myself more, or was more delighted or more interested, *and I can think* and talk of nothing else . . . For the Emperor *personally* I have conceived a *real* affection, and so I may truly say of the Prince. . . . I cannot say *how* pleasant and easy it is to live with him or how attached one becomes to him. I know *no* one who puts me more at my ease, or in whom involuntarily I should be more inclined to confide . . . in short, without *attempting* to do anything particular to *make* one like him, he has the power of *attaching* those to him who come near him, which is quite *incredible*.

The Queen warms the reader's heart by her excited and generous enjoyment of the visit. The Emperor had, however, attempted 'to do something particular' to make her like him, or so at least the observant Clarendon said to Greville, who consigned the report to his journal:

> She was charmed with the Emperor, who had made love to her, which he did with a tact which proved quite successful. He began this when he was in England, and the Queen was evidently mightily tickled by it, for She had never been made love to in her life, and never had conversed with a man of the world on a footing of equality; and as his love-making was of a character to flatter her vanity without alarming her virtue and modesty, She enjoyed the novelty of it without scruple or fear. After her visit She talked it over with C. and said it was very extraordinary and unaccountable but the Emperor knew about her from the time she was 12 years old and had told her where she had been, when he had seen her, and even what She wore!

The Emperor's information-service must have been very busy unearthing details of the gowns worn by the Queen years earlier. Clarendon's report is the more interesting because we know how Disraeli later insinuated himself into the Queen's good graces. In each case an adventurer, not wholly insincere, employed arts that may fairly be called un-English.

Now for a rapid summary of the aftermath. Disillusionment with the Emperor did not set in at once, but the *entente* soon ceased to be *cordiale*. Within two months of the visit Sebastopol fell. Napoleon and his people wanted peace. The Queen and her people did not. For one thing it was the French alone who had captured the fortress. The British had previously shown heroic courage, but now our troops were for the most part raw, or else embittered, and they refused to follow their officers. The Queen commented: 'The honour and glory of her dear Army is as *near* to her heart as almost anything, and she cannot *bear* the thought that the failure on the Redan should be our last *fait d'armes*, and it would cost her more than words can express to conclude peace with this as the end. However,' she adds with her usual good sense, 'what is best and wisest must be done'. To continue the war without our French ally would obviously not be good or wise; was the little British Army to advance from the Crimea towards Moscow? Peace was signed in March, 1856. Five months later the Queen wrote, not to the Emperor but to the Empress, complaining of the regrettable differences between the French and British Governments about the non-execution of the treaty. Relations became more and more shaky until in the following May the Emperor suggested himself for another visit. The proposal was not very welcome; but when in August he arrived with the Empress at Osborne in his yacht his personal charm and desire to please banished 'the very black cloud' hanging over the alliance and before he departed 'all was sunshine'.

A year later the royal pair made a return visit by yacht, and were received at Cherbourg. The Prince Consort avoided reviewing the French armed forces, the 'glorification' of which was directed, he considered, against England; the Queen avoided giving her usual kiss to Walewski's wife, whose liaison with the Emperor had become scandalously evident. Soon afterwards Napoleon's Italian campaign and annexation of Savoy excited disgust at Windsor; and then the Queen's enthusiasm for German unity enraged the Tuileries. During a private tour of England and Scotland in 1860 the Empress came to Windsor, and in 1868 the Queen visited her privately in Paris, though without seeing Napoleon, whom she did not meet again until he and the Empress landed here as dethroned refugees.

The Empress arrived six months before her husband, who was a prisoner in Prussian hands. The Queen called to express sympathy. When he arrived, he was given an invitation to Windsor, brought in person by the Prince of Wales. The Queen received him as a sovereign, at the door and with an embrace. Within two years he was dead; and henceforward her affection for the Empress was strengthened by their common widowhood.

A second bereavement reinforced the bond. The Prince Imperial, Eugénie's only child, went to Sandhurst and obtained his commission. He insisted upon fighting against the Zulus in 1879, and was killed serving the Queen. Her distress was made more acute by shame: a British fellow-officer had through loss of nerve abandoned the Prince to a fate from which he might have been saved. When the body was brought back, the Queen kneeled beside it in the *chapelle ardente* at Chiselhurst, and then from a window watched the funeral procession in which her four sons acted as pall-bearers. In the following August the Empress came to stay at Osborne, and gave the Queen 'a most splendid cross' carved from a single emerald which had been a wedding-present from the King of Spain. It was just twenty-five years previously, the Queen remarked in her journal, that she and Prince Albert had arrived in state and splendour at Paris and Saint-Cloud. Doubtless there was now much talk about those happier days; and I surmise – without any evidence – that the Queen then conceived the idea of the book about the two state visits. This was the year, 1880, in which she prepared it for the printer; and what purpose could be more likely than to give pleasure to the Empress?

The journals here reprinted remind us delightfully of her ebullience and capacity for pleasure – characteristics sometimes overlooked because of her later submergence in mourning. The ten days in France with the Prince, the Emperor and the Empress seem to have been the most enjoyable in the whole of her long, duty-laden life.

RAYMOND MORTIMER

Principal authorities quoted:

The Letters of Queen Victoria. (John Murray).

The Greville Memoirs. Edited by Lytton Strachey and Roger Fulford. (Macmillan).

Louis Napoleon and the Recovery of France, by F. A. Simpson. (Longmans Green).

The Life and Letters of the Fourth Earl of Clarendon, by Sir Herbert Maxwell. (Arnold).

A Vanished Victorian, by George Villiers. (Eyre & Spottiswoode).

Randall Davidson, by G. K. A. Bell. (Oxford University Press).

THE VISIT OF THE EMPEROR
AND EMPRESS OF THE FRENCH
TO THE QUEEN

Windsor Castle, Friday, April 13*th*, 1855

In the afternoon, after luncheon, arrived Queen
Amélie[1] with Clém.[2] She was most kind and most
discreet, and said she felt my kindness very deeply.
'*Je le sens plus que je ne puis le dire.*' I feel so much for
her. It made us both so sad to see her drive away in
a plain coach with four miserable post-horses, and to
think that this was the Queen of the French, who, six
years ago, was surrounded by the pomp and grandeur
which now belong to others; that in three more days
the Emperor of the French would be received with all
possible respect, pomp, and éclat, and that this same
reception attended her late husband here. Now *all* is
swept away; another dynasty reigns in that fickle
country!

The contrast was painful in the extreme. I have
been looking over my beautiful Album d'Eu,[3] which
brought all the past vividly back to my memory.

1. Queen Marie-Amélie, widow of King Louis-Philippe.
2. Her daughter, Princesse Clémentine, later Princess
Augustus of Saxe-Coburg-Gotha.
3. An album given to the Queen by King Louis-Philippe,
containing water-colour drawings by French artists of the
Château d'Eu and the surrounding country, and of the principal
events during the Queen's visit there in 1843.

[25]

Dull early, but became fine and very warm. We walked with the seven children to the stables, where we saw the Emperor's horses, fourteen, which he has sent over. Two French grooms were already walking about yesterday afternoon. The head groom is an Englishman, who was with the Emperor in England; and one of his grooms is a German, who was with him at Strasburg and Boulogne. The horses are fine. At eleven, service. After luncheon we went with all the children and Charles[1] (no one more interested than little Arthur[2]) all over the rooms, beginning with the Imperial couple's. (1) The Rubens Room, beautifully redecorated with very handsome crimson furniture, is the Empress's drawing-room; next to which is − (2) The Empress's bedroom, all crimson satin, with the fine old pictures and very handsome furniture, and a really beautiful bed. The top, with feathers, is the same which used to be in the state bedroom and belonged to George IV's bed, but the bedstead has been enlarged with a green front, on which is embroidered an eagle and LN and EI, with curtains of violet satin, upon which is placed some beautiful old

1. Prince Charles Leiningen, the Queen's half-brother, son of the Duchess of Kent by her first marriage to Emich Charles, Prince of Leiningen.
2. Prince Arthur, later Duke of Connaught.

embroidery. (3) The Empress's dressing-room, also hung with crimson satin and green satin furniture, with a handsome toilet. My gold things are to be put upon it. (4) The Emperor's bedroom, where the Emperor Nicholas[1] and poor King Louis-Philippe slept. The bed and furniture are of green velvet, very handsome; all little details are most carefully attended to, and very handsome. (5) The Zuccarelli Room, which is the Emperor's sitting-room. (6) The Vandyke Room, which looks magnificent, with green and yellow silk curtains and furniture – handsome tables, &c., and the two adjoining Tapestry Rooms, also beautifully done up, are the gentlemen and ladies' waiting-rooms.

Upstairs, the rooms for the attendants, though rather low, are nice and clean, with pretty chintz furniture and a very fine look-out. A great deal of new furniture has been got, though there was much fine old furniture in store, which has been usefully worked up.

Monday, April 16th

Foggy early. Heard my dear Albert had arrived safe at half-past ten. All is in a bustle, and excitement and expectation.

I have had such trouble with my toilette, dresses, bonnets, caps, mantillas, &c. &c. of every sort and

1. Emperor Nicholas I of Russia, who visited Windsor Castle in June 1844.

kind. Very fine, but intensely hot sun, which had succeeded the fog. Walked with Charles down to Frogmore to see Mama.

A really glorious day. All the children on the tip-top of expectation; dear little Arthur full of the Arch and the flags, and the Emperor, &c., and so excited, but most dear and sensible. Went over to the Empress's rooms, and saw her dressers, who, with other servants and many *fourgons*, arrived yesterday. Heard at luncheon that the Emperor had arrived at Dover at forty minutes past two. They had sailed at a quarter to ten. A thick fog. Drove out in the Park with Lady Canning[1] and Charles; dreadfully hot sun. Quantities of people walking and driving to Windsor, all for the event. We found Windsor so gay, so full – flags, preparations for the illuminations, and crowds who had already taken their places, who cheered me loudly as I drove up through the very handsome arch. The Guard arrived immediately afterwards.

News arrived from London at a quarter to five that the Emperor had reached London at the 'Bricklayers' Arms' at ten minutes to five [*sic*]. I hurried to be ready. Wore a light blue dress with shaded trimmings, and a pearl necklace; and at six went with George,[2] Charles (in uniform, as well as all the gentlemen), Vicky,[3] Bertie[4] (in full Highland dress, with a claymore) into the gallery, where were

1. Lady of the Bedchamber.
2. Prince George, Duke of Cambridge, the Queen's first cousin.
3. The Princess Royal.
4. The Prince of Wales.

assembled the whole Court and Officers of State and Household (the Duchess of Wellington[1] representing the Duchess of Sutherland[2]), Lady Ely[3] and Miss Seymour,[4] Lord Somers[5] and Sir F. Stovin[6] (who will be attached to the Emperor and Empress).

In a state of anxious expectation, we went over to the other side, where we waited in one of the Tapestry Rooms next the Guard Room. It seemed *very* long. At length, at a quarter to seven, we heard that the train had left Paddington. The expectation and agitation immense. The evening fine – bright. The crowd of anxious spectators lining the road seemed to move; – then came a groom, then we heard a gun; – and we moved towards the Staircase. Another groom came, we moved up to the door; then we saw the *avant-garde* of the Escort; then the cheers of the crowd burst forth. The outriders appeared – the doors opened – I stepped out, the Children and Princes close behind me; the band struck up *Partant pour la Syrie*,[7] the trumpet sounding – and the open carriage with the Emperor and Empress – Albert sitting opposite to them – drove up, and they got out. I cannot say what indescribable emotions filled me, how much it felt like a wonderful dream! These great meetings of

1 and 3. Ladies of the Bedchamber.
2. Mistress of the Robes.
4. The Hon. Mary Seymour, Maid of Honour.
5. Lord-in-Waiting.
6. Major-General Sir Frederick Stovin, Groom-in-Waiting.
7. The song, with words by the Emperor's mother, Queen Hortense of Holland, and music by M. Labord, adopted by Napoleon III as the French national air.

Sovereigns, surrounded by very exciting accompaniments, are always very agitating.

I advanced and embraced the Emperor, who received two salutes, on either cheek, from me, having first kissed my hand. I next embraced the very gentle, graceful, and evidently very nervous Empress. We presented each the Princes and our children (Vicky with very alarmed eyes making very low curtsies: the Emperor embraced Bertie), and then we went up the Grand Stairs, Albert leading the Empress, who in the most graceful manner refused to go first, but at length, with graceful reluctance, did so; the Emperor leading me – expressing his great gratification at being here and seeing me, and admiring Windsor. The Yeomen of the Guard were stationed on the Staircase and in the Vestibule. We went into the Throne Room, where we presented the five other Children, to whom they were very kind. We then stepped into the Reception Room, where I presented all the Ladies to the Empress and the Emperor, and where Albert presented our Gentlemen to the Emperor, and they introduced their attendants to us. We then conducted them to their apartments.

The Emperor was in uniform. He is extremely short; but with a head and bust which ought to belong to a much taller man. She is taller; was in a plain plaid silk dress and straw bonnet, with a black velvet mantilla. She is most graceful and pleasing, with a very charming kind expression.

We left them and hastened to our rooms. Everything had gone off beautifully. The reception had been

wonderfully enthusiastic. It took an hour and a half
going through London. But the fog had been fearful – the passage dangerous. The *Austerlitz* had got
aground; and if Captain Smithett had not been on board
as a pilot, the steamer, with its very valuable freight,
might have been in great danger. Our fleet, stationed
there to receive the Emperor, was not even seen!

At a quarter-past eight we went over to the Rubens
Room, where we found the Emperor and Empress,
and took them to the Throne Room, where were
Mama and the Princes. I presented Mama. We then
went into the Reception Room, where the company
was assembled. Dinner was announced, and we at
once went in; Albert going first with the Empress,
the Emperor leading me, and George leading Mama,
who sat on the other side of the Emperor, and George
to my left; Albert sat next the Empress, and Charles
on her other side.

We got on extremely well at dinner, and my great
agitation seemed to go off very early; the Emperor is
so very quiet: his voice is low and soft, and *il ne fait
pas de phrases*. The Emperor said that the first time he
had seen me was eighteen years ago, when I went for
the first time to prorogue Parliament, and that it
made a very deep impression upon him to see *une
jeune personne* in that position. He also mentioned his
having been a special constable on April 10th, 1848,[1]
and wondered whether I had known it. The war, and
the news, which arrived just as he did, of the opening

1. The Government had anticipated a Chartist insurrection
on April 10th.

of the fire from four hundred batteries,[1] were a subject of conversation also. He is very anxious about the siege: *'j'avoue que je crains un grand désastre, et c'est pour cela que je voudrais y aller,'* as he thought *'que nos généraux'* would take nothing upon themselves. I then observed upon the danger to which he might be exposed, how great the distance was, &c. . . . He added that there were dangers everywhere, though he admitted the distance was very great.

The Empress wore a wreath of pink chrysanthemums, and a grey silk dress trimmed with lace, underneath which there were little pink bows, and pink bows trimmed round the body; a necklace and brooch of emeralds and diamonds, no earrings, and beautiful bracelets. The profile and the line of the throat and shoulders are very beautiful, the expression charming and gentle, quite delightful. The pictures of Winterhalter are very like her. The hair light brown, the face very pale, the mouth and teeth lovely. She does not bear standing well. She is very lively and talkative when at her ease, which she got soon to be with me.

Two of the ladies, the Princesse d'Essling and Madame de Malaret, could not appear, their things not having arrived. Four of the gentlemen also only arrived after dinner, having been detained by the fog on board their ship.

I wore a yellow dress trimmed with white blonde, my opal diadem and opals.

1. The siege of Sebastopol, which had begun in the autumn of 1854, was still in progress.

The arrival of the Emperor and Empress of the French at Windsor Castle, April 16th, 1855
G. H. Thomas

The Emperor Napoleon III. Photograph by Meyer frères.

We broke up at half-past eleven, and accompanied them to their rooms.

Tuesday, April 17th

Splendid weather. Albert went at nine to fetch the Emperor, and brought him to the White Room, where we were with the four eldest children, George and Charles. Albert sat in his usual place; the Emperor next to him, and I next to the Emperor. He was very quiet and amiable, and easy to get on with. We talked of the war; in particular of Sebastopol, the difficulties, &c. He said: *Il faut tâcher de faire une diversion.'* He lamented over the King of Prussia.[1] We went out through the courtyard. It was about ten minutes to ten – a beautiful morning – with the Emperor leading me – he walks slow, – George and Charles. We walked by the Kennel, where we looked at the dogs – through the farm, by the hen-house, on to Frogmore, where we paid Mama a short visit.

Nothing can be more civil or amiable, or more well-bred, than the Emperor's manner, – so full of tact. We walked up to the Castle the straight way from Frogmore. He admired the grass very much, and said (as all foreigners do) that you could never get that on the Continent. During almost the whole time of the walk, the war and his plans were discussed, the

1. The attitude of Frederick William IV towards the Anglo-French alliance and the Crimean War was by no means helpful.

different means of making a diversion, the fortifications of Kamiesch, &c. &c. There are now four
hundred gun mortars (*bouches à feu*), each with a
thousand rounds of ammunition, firing on Sebastopol,
and this can go on for *huit jours et huit nuits*; but he
said that if then the town is not destroyed, and the
breach is not made, *il faut se retirer*. This is a very
alarming thing indeed.

It was most interesting to hear him and Albert
discuss all these matters. He said that if Austria, after
all she had done, and after going so far as she had
done, was *not* to join in the war, *ce ne serait pas
loyal*.

Home by half-past eleven. Albert went over to the
Emperor's apartment, where there was to be a pre-
liminary discussion respecting the war; and at twelve
I went to the Empress, who received me in the Rubens
Room. She was very plainly and prettily dressed, in
light blue silk, high up to the throat, trimmed with
narrow black lace (many small trimmings of it). I
found her quite at her ease with me, and talking away
with Spanish liveliness and vivacity. She takes the
warmest interest in the war, and is all for the Emperor's going. She sees no greater danger for him
there than elsewhere, in fact than in Paris. She was
sure that '*il aura de bonnes raisons à donner à votre
Majesté*' for doing so; that '*il faut étonner les Français;
il ne faut jamais leur caisser le dernier mot; c'est
ainsi que l'Empereur a toujours fait;* that she was
seldom alarmed for him except when he went out
quite alone of a morning; that on the occasion of that

conspiracy[1] two years ago there certainly was great
danger, but the police, being aware of it, had pre-
tended to belong to the conspirators, and this enabled
them to be taken at the very moment when they
intended to make the attempt. She is full of courage
and spirit, and yet so gentle; with such innocence and
enjouement, that the *ensemble* is most charming. With
all this great liveliness, she has the prettiest and most
modest manner. She spoke much of Spain, and with
sorrow of the misfortunes of that country, and of the
unhappy Queen.[2] I remained about half-an-hour, when
Mama came to see her.

At two the Emperor and Empress came over to join
us at luncheon, the same as at breakfast, the four
younger children coming in at dessert. Leopold[3] was
presented, and was good, allowing the Emperor, and
afterwards the Empress, to kiss him. I mentioned the
two lithographs of the Empress in her Spanish dress,
on horseback, upon which she said, that one had been
done *'par le Prince de Joinville.'*[4] The Emperor then
asked me *'où était la Reine Marie-Amélie?'* and on my
saying 'In England,' he said that he last year wrote to
Uncle Leopold,[5] saying that, if the voyage back from
Spain was too long for her, he hoped that she would
come through France (the family are exiled), *'et si votre
Majesté veut bien le lui répéter, j'en serais bien content'*.

1. One of several attempts made at various times on the
Emperor's life.
2. Isabella II.
3. Prince Leopold, later Duke of Albany.
4. François Ferdinand, third son of King Louis-Philippe.
5. Leopold, King of the Belgians.

They had to hasten off to receive a deputation from the City. At four we all set off for the Review, which was a most brilliant, and beautiful, and exciting affair. The Court was full of carriages and horses with brilliant caparisons. Our grooms, and the Emperor's *piqueurs* in dark green, with gold lace, countless uniforms, &c., all looked so bright and gay. In the first carriage (we drove from the Emperor's side of the Castle) were the Empress (whom I always made get in and walk first), I, Bertie, Vicky, and dear little Arthur; Albert, the Emperor, George, and all the military gentlemen on horseback. Alice[1] Alfred,[2] Charles, and Madame Walewska[3] were in the second carriage; Lenchen,[4] Louise,[5] the Duchess of Wellington, and Princesse d'Essling in the third – many more following. The crowd, in the Long Walk, of people on foot and horseback, was tremendous, and the excitement and cheering beyond description. They squeezed round the Emperor when we came to the gates, and rode across the grass to where the Review was to be, in such a way that I grew very nervous, as he rode along on a very fiery beautiful chestnut called 'Philips', and was so exposed. He rides extremely well, and looks well on horseback, as he sits high.

The Emperor rode down the line with Albert and George, we following, as well as the second carriage.

1. Princess Alice, later Grand Duchess of Hesse.
2. Prince Alfred (Affie), later Duke of Edinburgh.
3. Wife of the French Ambassador in London.
4. Princess Helena, later Princess Christian of Schleswig-Holstein.
5. Princess Louise, later Duchess of Argyll.

After that we were stationed to see them pass by, in slow and quick time: the Blues, 2nd Life Guards, Carabineers, and a troop of Horse Artillery, Lord Cardigan commanding, on the very chestnut horse he rode at Balaklava, and in a great state of excitement. They afterwards manœuvred, and the Artillery was seen to great advantage. The Emperor, who rode several times up to our carriage, and the Princes, rode about and charged with the Cavalry, &c. The whole concluded, as it began, with the royal salute. We then returned as we came, accompanied by an escort; and the enthusiasm, the crowd of excited people and riders, were quite indescribable. I never remember any excitement like it. It was at moments almost alarming, and there were numbers of terrified ladies standing on the road, clasping one another for fear of being ridden over. The Emperor, Albert, George, and the very numerous suite rode immediatly behind us. The whole was again quite a triumph.

We got home by half-past six. I had been suffering all day more or less with headache, from the heat of the sun and the excitement. The evening was very fine, though there was a cold wind. Very little time left for dressing, or indeed for anything; the contents of [despatch] boxes all remain unread and unsigned.

At a little before eight, we went over to the Emperor's apartments, leaving the Royal Family in the Throne Room (the Duchess of Cambridge and Mary[1] having come) and the suite in the small room adjoining.

1. Princess Mary of Cambridge.

[37]

The Empress was in white tarlatan, embroidered with lilies of the valley; splendid pearls round her neck, and pearls in her hair. I presented the Duchess of Cambridge and Mary. Mama of course to dinner.

Leading in the same. Comte Walewski[1] sat to my left, and the Duchess of Cambridge next the Emperor. He gave me a telegraphic despatch to read, which had come from Vienna, in which Austria *'consentirait à faire la guerre'* unless the Russian fleet remained the same as before the war (incredible and impossible), added to some other conditions which were worth consideration. The Emperor, while condemning the absurd notion of *'le chiffre de la flotte'* remaining the same, considered that it was *'un pas en avant,'* Austria having spoken of going to war. I spoke to him of those flattering letters from Comte Nesselrode to Baron Seebach which he had communicated to us (a week or ten days ago), and observed on the desire and hope there had been, and still was, on the Continent, that our Alliance could be broken. He said that the Russians at Paris had tried, and with some success, to make their party in France.[2] And indeed a good many other people believe that this question *'ne regardait que l'Angleterre, et que cela ne regardait pas la*

1. French Ambassador in London.
2. Count Nesselrode, the Russian Chancellor, had written to Baron von Seebach, the Saxon Minister in Paris, praising the Emperor's character and his qualities as a sovereign, but also advising Seebach to make it clear to the Emperor, directly as well as through others in high places, that the Tsar had no intention of reducing his armed forces as a condition of peace being established in the Crimea.

France; c'était bien habile d'eux et une grande difficulté pour moi'. He talked of the Empress, whom I praised very much.

After dinner Vicky appeared, looking very nice in light blue, and her hair out of her face. I wore a white dress trimmed with convolvuluses and blonde, and the same flowers in the hair. After the gentlemen came in, and some little *cercleing*, we went into the music-room (Waterloo Room), where the company passed by – I naming them to the Empress, and Albert to the Emperor. After this, the dancing began – a quadrille – I dancing with the Emperor, who dances with great dignity and spirit, and Albert opposite, with the Empress; George with Vicky. A valse followed: then another quadrille, in which George danced with the Empress, the Emperor with Mary, and Albert with Countess Walewska. It was followed by a reel, in which Vicky danced very nicely; then a valse, which the Emperor also danced well and quietly, with Vicky, whom he asked to dance with him, which frightened her very much. I joined in the valse with George. Lastly came a quadrille, in which I danced with the Duc de Bassano,[1] and Albert with the Comtesse de Montebello.[2] Really to think that I, the grand-daughter of George III, should dance with the Emperor Napoleon, nephew to our great enemy, now my nearest and most intimate ally, in the Waterloo Room too – and this ally, only six years ago, an exile, poor, comparatively little known, living in this

1. See p. 46.
2. See p. 45.

country, seems incredible. We went to supper – the Emperor leading me, and Albert leading the Empress. Her manner is the most perfect thing I have ever seen, – so gentle and graceful and kind, the curtsey so charming, and so modest and retiring withal. Over by half-past twelve. Vicky behaved extremely well, making beautiful curtsies, and was very much praised by the Emperor and Empress, whom Vicky raves about.

Wednesday, April 18*th*

The same brilliant weather. Breakfast as yesterday. The Duchess of Cambridge and Mary were the additions to our party. The Emperor took the greatest notice of Arthur, who is quite at his ease with him, and said: '*Je suis bien malheureux parce que l'Impératrice a perdu son cœur pour le Prince Arthur.*' During breakfast the Emperor received a telegraphic despatch announcing the death of his Minister of Marine, which grieved him. '*Pauvre homme,*' he said, '*cela me fait bien de la peine,*' adding that he had not expected it, though the Minister had been very ill, and that he was an able man.

At half-past ten we walked out with the Emperor, George and Charles, first round the Terrace, and then over the Stables. He said that it was a very extraordinary thing that he was going to name his new Minister of Marine '*de Windsor*'. He means to name Admiral Hamelin. We were home at eleven, and at half-past, Albert went to join the Emperor at the conference, or *conseil de guerre*, which was to be held in the Emperor's apartments, and at which Lords Clarendon, Palmerston, Panmure, Hardinge, and Cowley,[1] Maréchal Vaillant,[2] Comte Walewski, and Sir J. Burgoyne,[3] were to be present.

I rested. Despatches had come from the Crimea, but nothing very new. At one, the dear sweet Empress came over to see me. I met her in the corridor, and presented the three governesses to her, and then took her into my room, where she was pleased with all the pictures. She wore a light greyish *chinée* silk with black flowers, and, as usual, not an ornament, – only a black lace handkerchief round her throat, and her pretty hair done in that simple way, combed back, but not what used to be called *à l'Impératrice*. She stayed for nearly half-an-hour.

At two, I went over to her room, but the *conseil* was still going on, though they had been told that all was ready for luncheon. After waiting a little while, the Empress went and asked and told Lord Cowley how late it was. Then, after waiting a little while longer, she advised me to go to tell them. '*Je n'ose entrer, mais votre Majesté le peut. Cela vous regarde.*' So I went through the Emperor's room (the council room

1. Lord Clarendon, Secretary for Foreign Affairs; Lord Palmerston, Prime Minister; Lord Panmure, Secretary for War; Lord Hardinge, Commander-in-Chief of the Army; Lord Cowley, British Ambassador in Paris.

2. French Minister of War.

3. Lieut.-Gen. Sir J. Burgoyne, attached to Lord Raglan's staff in the Crimea.

adjoined his bedroom) and knocked, and at last stepped in, and asked what we should do. The Emperor and Albert got up, and said they would come. However, they did not do so, and after further *pourparler* with the Empress, and looking at her dress and splendid jewels, many of which were Crown jewels, which the Empress has had reset, we agreed to dress our heads, and lunch in that way, and at about half-past two we all (except the Duchess of Cambridge) lunched.

The Emperor and Empress had a table covered with toys they had brought for the children: a doll and trousseau, beautiful soldiers for Arthur, a panorama, games, a beautiful little picture of a dog *en Gobelin* for Vicky, and, finally, two beautiful models of the nine-pounders the Emperor has himself invented, and which he showed off with great pleasure. He is so very quiet, good-natured and unassuming and natural, if one may use such a word.

Then came a great scramble for dressing. At length, at nearly half-past three, we went over in the usual manner to the Throne Room. The Empress was seated at the other end opposite to me with her attendants, and Vicky and Bertie on one side, and the Duchess of Cambridge with Alice and Affie on the other. The forms having been gone through, Albert and George went out of the room and fetched in the Emperor, who walked between them, and was in his General's uniform, with white shorts. We all rose and remained standing. I then announced to him that he was elected a Knight of the Most Noble Order of the Garter. Albert then buckled on the Garter round his leg, which I thought took longer than usual, during which the Bishop of Oxford read the admonition, and when he had done, the Emperor put his foot on the cushion, and I pulled the garter through the knot. He kissed my hand and I kissed him. We then put the ribbon on, and the Emperor put first the wrong arm through. We were *all* nervous, including myself. This done, he kissed my hand again and I again embraced him; after which he shook hands with all the Knights, and sat down in the arm-chair of state, which had been placed for him. The Knights were called over, and then, I taking the Emperor's arm, and Albert the Empress's, we walked through the rooms to the Emperor's apartments. As we were going along, the Emperor said: *'Je remercie bien votre Majesté; c'est un lien de plus; j'ai prêté serment de fidélité à votre Majesté et je le garderai soigneusement.'* He added a little later: *'C'est un grand événement pour moi, et j'espère pouvoir prouver ma reconnaissance à votre Majesté et à son pays.'* These words are valuable from a man like him, who is not profuse in phrases, and who is very steady of purpose.

We then left them, the Emperor wishing to walk with Albert, and the Empress feeling the cold. I drove with the Duchess of Cambridge, Mary, and Charles. Very cold. On coming back, I ran out to meet Albert and the Emperor, who were walking on the Terrace, and had been taking a long walk in the Slopes. We went in together. He admires Windsor excessively: in short, everything that is English he admires so much.

[43]

Dinner was to be at half-past seven. Such a scramble always, so much to do and think of. We went over to the Emperor's and Empress's apartments: they met us already in the Throne Room, and we went in at once. The Empress wore the pearl diadem again, and a white dress trimmed with blonde. I wore a white and gold brocade, a diamond diadem, the Koh-i-noor, and the Indian pearls. Mama sat on the Emperor's other side, and George on my left; Charles next the Empress, and the Duchess of Cambridge on his other side. The Empress talked and was particularly lively.

I showed the Emperor a telegraphic account I had received from Vienna; the Austrians make propositions. We heard yesterday that the batteries had maintained the superiority over the enemy, and were advancing nearer. The Emperor talked of the shocking refugees in London;[1] he said he thought that when assassination was loudly and openly advocated, they ought not to enjoy hospitality. He said that Victor Hugo, whom he knew, who had written in his praise, had dined at his table, and wished to be Minister, had become, and was now, one of the very worst of his assailants. We talked of the various attempts on me, which he thought were too atrocious as against a woman. As for himself, he said he had the same opinion as his uncle had had, which was, that when there was a conspiracy that was known, and you could take your precautions, there was no danger; but that

1. Those who fled from Paris following Napoleon III's *coup d'état* in 1851.

when a fanatic chose to attack you, and to sacrifice his own life, you could do little or nothing to prevent it. This is very true.[1]

We talked of the Revolution in 1848, and the horrors in June. He said he had met George driving, and that George had said, half-jokingly: '*Est-ce qu'on se bat pour vous à Paris?*' that he had answered, Oh! there was no question of him; '*et cependant déjà on se battait pour moi alors!*' Speaking of the want of liberty attaching to our position, he said the Empress felt this much, and called the Tuileries '*une belle prison*'. He himself felt this deeply. '*J'ai pleuré de chaudes larmes en quittant l'Angleterre.*'

I want now to speak of the attendants of the Emperor and Empress. First, the ladies. The Princesse d'Essling, *Grande Maîtresse*, past forty, with the remains of good looks, quiet, and ladylike. Her husband, who behaved ill towards her, was the son of Marshal Massena. The Comtesse de Montebello, pleasing, rather nice-looking, and gentle. She was the daughter of the Marquis de Villeneuve, and her grandmother was one of Marie-Antoinette's ladies, and guillotined.

Madame la Baronne de Malaret, tall, rather handsome, very Russian-looking, and ladylike. She is the daughter of the Marquis de Ségur, and her mother

1. On April 29th, a few days after the Emperor's return to Paris, while riding in the Champs-Elysées, he was shot at by an Italian, Giacomo Pianori. The assassin, who was close to the Emperor, fired twice, but missed. Revenge for the French occupation of Rome was said to be Pianori's motive. The Emperor showed no signs of disquietude, and rode on at a foot's pace to the Empress, who was driving in the Bois de Boulogne.

[45]

was the daughter of Rostopchin, who set fire to Moscow. These two are *Dames du Palais*. All three wear the Empress's *chiffre* to a ribbon on their shoulder.

The gentlemen: Maréchal Vaillant, *Grand Maréchal* and *Ministre de la Guerre*; tall and very large, quite in the style of Lablache,[1] with small fine features, and a charming, amusing, clever and honest old man, who is a universal favourite. The Duc de Bassano, *Grand Chambellan*, tall, quiet, and gentlemanlike, was a long time on the diplomatic staff at Brussels, and married the daughter of Madame d'Hoogvorst. The Général Comte de Montebello, an aide-de-camp, was here during the camp at Chobham — a good sort of man, about forty-four or forty-five: he is the husband of the Comtesse Montebello, and is the son of Marshal Lannes. Colonel Fleury, also aide-de-camp and first *écuyer de l'Empereur*, commands the Guides and manages the stables, and is most devoted to the Emperor; about forty, tall and soldier-like. Le Comte Edgar Ney, youngish, but bald, an *élégant* and gentlemanlike, the youngest son of Marshal Ney. Le Marquis de Toulongeon, *officier d'ordonnance*, a quiet, unassuming man, about thirty. Le Comte Charles Tascher de la Pagerie, *Chambellan* of the Empress. His father, who was first-cousin to the Empress Joséphine, settled in Germany, married a Princesse Leyen, and this son was born there, and is completely German in appearance and manner. His father is also

1. Luigi Lablache, the famous bass, who taught the Queen singing.

about the Empress. Count Tascher is an elderly man. Le Colonel Rouher, aide-de-camp of Maréchal Vaillant, is a quiet and very retiring young man.

I had some conversation with Maréchal Vaillant after dinner. He is very much against the Emperor's going to the Crimea, and hoped I had spoken to him. I said: *'J'ai osé faire quelques observations.' 'Mon Dieu, oser!'* he said. *'Quand on est ensemble il faut parler nettement.'* The danger, he said, was very great. The plan of the Emperor was a very good one, and if any other general executed it and failed, it would not signify; but the Emperor, the Sovereign – that was a risk which was too serious to be run. Even for us, he added, though it could not injure us in the way it might France, still that *un échec* would be very serious too; *'vous êtes dans le même bateau;'* adding that he thought there was great danger to France in the Emperor's absence. He hoped that the *conseil* had, however, had some effect on the Emperor: *'Le Prince votre époux a été bien net,'* and had always brought people back to the point when they digressed. The Emperor told me, if it had not been for Albert, nothing would have been done.

Colonel Fleury, to whom I afterwards spoke, expressed the greatest alarm at the Emperor's going, and said: *'Nous espérons que votre Majesté pourra empêcher ce voyage;'* that it would be of the greatest danger to France; that he was sure this could not be a matter of indifference to us; that the risk was immense; and that this was the opinion of all who had any weight in France. *'L'édifice n'est pas encore si sûr,'* he said; adding, '*C'est la prière*' of all who wished for the welfare of France, that this expedition should be prevented.

There was a concert, only orchestral, in the music-room. Everybody was seated when we came in, and I sat between the Emperor and Empress. Every one was in full dress, and the Emperor in his General's uniform, with boots and the ribbon and star of the Garter on. He is short, and, as I before said, the bust and shoulders broad, and the head large, indicating that he ought to have been tall. His profile is good; the eyes are light blue, deep set and very peculiar, with a melancholy cast, an expression mild and gentle, as well as determined. His hair is rather lighter than ours, not at all grey, neither is he bald. He has no whiskers, but great moustaches, with very long straight ends to them, like the poor Duke of Genoa's, and a long *royale*. The neck is short. Altogether he is remarkable looking. The manners are particularly good, easy, quiet, and dignified, as if he had been born a king's son, and brought up for the place. He does not care at all for music.

The company went by as they did the preceding evening, and afterwards we went into St George's Hall, where (as yesterday) the supper was. I had a little talk with good Lord Aberdeen,[1] who does not quite like this visit and its associations, and seems to think that it affords grave reflections for the future.

1. Lord Aberdeen had retired as Prime Minister earlier in the year and had been succeeded by Lord Palmerston.

The Empress Eugénie, from a pencil drawing by Queen Victoria

The visit of Queen Victoria and the Emperor Napoleon to the Italian Opera at Covent Garden, April 19th, 1855.   L. Haghe.

Another bright, fine morning. Breakfast as on the preceding days. After the Duchess of Cambridge, Mary and George, had taken leave, and Charles had left the room, the Emperor said: '*Je vais maintenant, si votre Majesté le permet, lui lire ma réponse à l'Adresse de la Cité;* which, he had already told me yesterday, he would do, '*afin de savoir si vous aviez quelques observations à faire*'. He then read it to us in French, and we could only assent to everything in it, as it is an admirable speech; and as everything he says or writes is the result of mature reflection, and is always recurred to and remembered, it is of great importance. He then asked to read it in English (into which he had had it translated), asking us to correct his pronunciation, which we did, though it required but little; he also asked our advice about one or two expressions. He did all this very naturally and frankly.

At eleven we went over to the Emperor's and Empress's apartments, and then got into the carriages. The children had all gone an hour before us; the Emperor and Empress being in the carriage (the same pony-barouche in which they arrived) with us, everything being just the same as on their arrival, only no one being in uniform; the guard of honour, the escort, the band playing *Partant pour la Syrie*, &c. I cannot say *why*, but their departure made me so

D

melancholy. I was near crying. Passing through the rooms, the hall, and down the stairs, with all its state guards, and the fine old yeomen, the very melancholy tune which *Partant pour la Syrie* is, the feeling that all about which there had been so much excitement, trouble, anxiety, and expectation, was past, the doubt-fulness of the future – all made me, I know not why, quite *wehmüthig*; and I hear that the Empress was equally sad at going away from Windsor. She said, looking at the Round Tower, '*C'est si beau, c'est si poétique; il n'y a rien de si beau'*. The Emperor admired it also very much.

We found another band at the South-Western station [Windsor], also at the station at Nine Elms, and in the quadrangle at Buckingham Palace. We got into the train, and Charles was in the saloon with us. We talked in the carriage of Charles I and Louis XVI, and the Emperor recited some German verses to one of the national tunes, *Studentenlieder* (*Student's Songs*) which he admires so much.

An immense crowd in London (of course an escort) and everywhere a most enthusiastic reception, hearty in the extreme. We took them up the staircase lead-ing to their side, along the corridor, to their apart-ments, where after a few minutes we left them. The Emperor pointed out to me, from the window of the Empress's saloon (the same window at which we showed ourselves on returning from the opening of the Exhibition, May 1st, 1851; from which we saw the Funeral of the poor Duke of Wellington, Novem-ber 18th, 1852, and from which we saw the Guards

depart,[1] February 28th, last year), the corner in the
Green Park, from which he saw me going to prorogue
Parliament in August 1837.

We went to see them before they went to the City.
The Empress looked lovely, in a light green-silk dress
trimmed with flounces of Brussels lace, a shawl to
match, no ornament whatever, and a white bonnet. It
was most elegant and pretty. Albert admired it
extremely. Altogether I am delighted to see how
much he likes her and admires her, as it is so seldom
that I see him do so with any woman. We saw them
drive away, in full state, just as when I go, with a long
row of carriages, and the cream-coloured horses in the
one in which the Imperial couple were. They passed
straight down the Mall through crowds of enthusiastic
people, the brilliant carriages and glittering escort of
the Life Guards having a beautiful effect. We gazed
till they were out of sight; but the crowd remained all
day before the Palace. While we were at luncheon we
heard that they had reached the City in safety – a great
relief, though I dreaded nothing.

Albert was engaged the whole afternoon in writing
a Memorandum on the Council of yesterday, and
elucidating the intended propositions. About half-past
four we heard cheering, saw people running across the
Park, and I saw the Imperial cortège returning along
Piccadilly, going to the Embassy to receive the *corps
diplomatique*. Walked a little with Charles in the
garden, and shortly after we came home at ten
minutes past six. Saw the Emperor and Empress

1. For the Crimea.

return – a fine sight again, escort, guard of honour, trumpets sounding. All this, with the splendid day, and the thousands of people, produced a most exciting effect, like the time of the Coronation, and the day of the opening of the Exhibition.

I went to see them with the children, and found them much pleased, everything having gone off so well. The Empress gave Vicky her beautiful watch of rubies and diamonds, with a beautiful little chain, seal, and watch-key to it. It was so kind of her. Vicky was in ecstasies. Arthur is an immense pet of both, and is excessively fond of the Emperor in his little quiet way.

We dined at a quarter to eight in the usual dining-room, with all our suites. The Emperor, Albert, and all the gentlemen were in uniform. The Empress wore a white net dress over white, with narrow blonde trimmings, and a diadem of emeralds and diamonds; I a blue and gold dress, with a diadem of diamonds, and very large Indian rubies. The Emperor, as a matter of course, always leads me, and always sits to my right; and Albert always leads the Empress, and sits to her left – we two ladies sitting just opposite to each other in the middle. I have, I think, quite forgotten to mention that Lady Ely and Miss Seymour are in attendance on the Empress, and Lord Somers, Sir F. Stovin, and Lord Alfred Paget, on the Emperor.

Maréchal Vaillant, who is a charming old man, and most amusing, sat next to me. The Emperor understands and speaks German perfectly. '*J'ai fait mes études en Allemagne, en Bavière,*' he said. He knows many pieces of German poetry by heart, and he seems to like to dwell upon those which have some '*Be-deutung*' (special significance) for him. He asked me several times whether I would come to Paris – to which I replied, Certainly, with pleasure, only that I could not promise beforehand, not being mistress of my time and actions. He said: '*Voilà ce que je voudrais; prendre Sébastopol, et puis recevoir votre Majesté à Paris.*' He always repeats his determination to go, if the negotiations end in nothing, and that '*cela sera très-court*'. The [1855] Exhibition building at Paris, he told me, he certainly had built with the intention of its being capable of holding a number of troops in case of any rising in Paris. He has had macadam laid down in almost all the streets, to prevent the people from taking up the pavement as hitherto, '*pour en faire des barricades*'.

We assembled in the gallery before starting for the Opera (in state), and just as we were ready to go, the Emperor upset his cup of coffee over his cocked hat, which caused great amusement.

We started at twenty minutes past nine, with escort and a number of carriages. Never did I see such enormous crowds at night, all in the highest good humour. We literally drove through a sea of human beings, cheering and pressing near the carriage. The streets were really beautifully illuminated, and many N.E.V.A.'s, which the Emperor said, curiously enough, made 'Neva,' the river on which St Petersburg is built. The coincidence seemed to strike him, for he said that already at Boulogne he had observed it.

When we arrived at the Opera House, Albert, as

usual, led the Empress, and the Emperor me; and when we entered I led the Emperor forward, and indicated, as much as I could, that *he* was the principal person on that occasion. The applause generally was very marked, for him especially so. They played first, *Partant pour la Syrie*, and then sang *God Save the Queen*. The second act of *Fidelio* followed. After this *God Save the Queen* was sung, and *Partant pour la Syrie* played. The whole stage was opened out, and two military bands stationed on it, which had a very fine effect. The Emperor told me, that after our marriage in 1840, when we went in state to Covent Garden, he asked for a box, and with difficulty got one, and afterwards they made him pay 40 l. for it, '*que je trouvais pourtant beaucoup*'. On this night I hear one person gave 100 l. for a box!

I reminded the Emperor that I had met him at a public breakfast, which was given at a villa at Fulham, for the benefit of the baths and washhouses, in 1848. Home as we came, with the same immense crowds. There was a supper in the bow library. We all remained talking for a little while. The Emperor had received more news from Sebastopol, which he hoped sounded favourable, but Albert was doubtful, and the Emperor said: '*J'ai bien peur que le Prince n'ait raison.*' All over by twelve.

The weather continued fine, which, it seems, is generally the case with the Emperor, as he told me, as well as with me. We discovered that it was his birthday, his forty-seventh, and though not fêted or taken any public notice of, we felt we could not do otherwise than take private notice of it. Consequently, when we went along the corridor to meet him, I wished him joy. He seemed for a moment to forget, and then smiled, kissed my hand, and thanked me, and I gave him a pencil. The Emperer told us a story of his having forgotten the time (when he was formerly in England), and having been shut up for two hours nearly, at night, in the Park. We had some further discussion about the war, and the Emperor spoke of the great mistake of Sebastopol not having been attempted to be taken after Alma, and of the way in which the Duke of Wellington stormed Badajoz. Albert's Memorandum could not be shown, as it was with Lord Palmerston, but Sir J. Burgoyne's answer, a letter from Lord Palmerston, and some other papers, were looked at.

The Empress was touched to tears when I gave her a bracelet with my hair. '*Oh, cela de la part de votre Majesté!*' showing how much she valued my kind *égards* and treatment in private as an equal. The Emperor was also very much pleased at Arthur's giving him two violets, the violet being the flower of the Bonapartes.

We started for the Crystal Palace[1] about twenty minutes past eleven, with the whole party (the Emperor and Empress with us). The Empress had a lilac dress on, trimmed with small trimmings of black lace, and a white chip bonnet; and I, a white dress with lilac flowers, and a white bonnet. Crowds everywhere; as we went along many cries of *'Vive l'Empereur!'* *'Vive l'Impératrice!'* and sometimes even *'Vive le Hemperor'* in cockney French.

The Emperor had just received despatches before we set out, and read them in the carriage, communicating some from the Crimea to Albert, and asking him to put them into one of his boxes which he had with him. Albert gave him his excellent Memorandum – with which he was pleased – to read.

The complete identity of interests facilitates all communications, and produces a feeling of friendship between the nations, and will do the same between the Emperor and ourselves, if he continues to behave with the same frankness and sincerity that he has done since the beginning of the war.

The Crystal Palace was empty when we arrived, and we were able to go quietly through the nave, and through all the courts. They were delighted with it, and much surprised. The Alhambra delighted the Empress, who is so fond of her own country. We stepped on to the balcony to look at the gardens and the beautiful view. The crowds assembled below were quite enormous, and the cheering very enthusiastic

1. The Great Exhibition of 1851 had been transferred from Hyde Park to Sydenham in 1854.

for each of us, my beloved Albert being asked for and warmly received. The dear Empress always puts herself in the background. She went in a Bath-chair part of the time, feeling a good deal tired.

We had luncheon with our whole party in our private apartments, in a room very prettily decorated for the purpose. Charles sat on my other side, and Count Walewski on the other side of the Empress. Albert got on famously with the Empress, and so did I with the Emperor, who is *very* fascinating; he is so quiet and gentle, and has such a soft pleasant voice. He is besides so simple and plain-spoken in all he says, and so devoid of all phrases, and has a good deal of poetry, romance, and *Schwärmerei* in his composition, which makes him peculiarly attractive. He is a most extraordinary, mysterious man, whom one feels excessively interested in watching and knowing. There is great dignity and tact in his manner. He always does the right thing, and behaves as if he had been all his life an Emperor! All he says is the result of deep reflection; and he sees in trifles and ordinary occurrences meanings and forebodings which no one else would find out.

While Albert took the Emperor for a moment into the garden, I remained sitting and talking with the Empress, and we came to the subject of the Emperor's journey to the Crimea and the anxiety it caused us; and then we talked of Prince Napoleon,[1] who, she said, had gone to the Crimea *'pour se laver,'* but that, as the Emperor had feared, it had done just the contrary, as

1. Son of King Jérôme Bonaparte and cousin of Napoleon III.

he had made himself very unpopular; that he was very clever, *'mais il tourne son esprit au mal'*; that it never would do to leave him behind at Paris during the Emperor's absence; that old Jérôme[1] was also not to be trusted, *'quoiqu'il soit très-bien pour les formes'*.

We were interrupted in the middle of the conversation by the return of the Emperor and Albert. We then walked through the transept, now densely crowded with people, on to the balcony again, to see the fountains play (for the first time), which they did most successfully. The effect is really beautiful. Afterwards we walked all through the transept, where there were between 30,000 and 40,000 people, all in perfect order, and cheering very loudly, on to an *estrade* where we sat down for a few minutes. It was in the same place where we were at the opening. There were two banners behind us, with N and V. This over, we went away. Nothing could have succeeded better; but I own I felt anxious as we passed along through the multitude of people, who after all were very close to us. I felt as I walked at the Emperor's arm, that I was possibly a protection for him. All thoughts of nervousness for myself were past. I thought only of him, and so it is, Albert says, when one forgets oneself one loses that great and foolish nervousness.

Great crowds, as before, on our way back. We came home at four; and Arthur appeared in his uniform, which delighted the Emperor, and he took him on his knee and played with him. At five I drove with the Emperor and Empress to Gloucester House, where

1. Brother of Napoleon I and father of the above.

I introduced them to the Duchess of Gloucester, who was very '*aimable*' too. Aunt Gloucester gave the Empress a nosegay. We only stayed a few minutes, and then came back, I taking them to their apartments.

The Emperor rode out with Albert afterwards, which he had so very much wished to do, but only for half-an-hour, and at a great pace. There was to be a meeting with the Ministers at six, to come at last to an agreement as to what was to be done. I followed at a little after six, and found the Emperor, Albert, Maréchal Vaillant, Lords Clarendon, Palmerston, and Panmure, in Albert's sitting-room. They were reading when I came in, and I seated myself on the sofa next the Emperor; Albert sitting on a chair next to me; then Lord Panmure and Lord Palmerston; the Maréchal on the sofa opposite to me (the large writing-table being between us); and Lord Clarendon on a chair next to him. I think it was one of the most interesting things I ever was present at, and one which I would not have missed for the world. The result of the whole was the paper which I annex,[1] and which was signed the next morning by our respective War Ministers. It had been drawn up, first, by Albert, as a résumé of his Memorandum, and was read over several times by the Emperor in English, and by the Ministers, and then finally *rédigé* by Albert according to the Emperor's wishes, as it now is. The principal alteration was in the term, 'two armies of operation,' which had originally been called 'covering army' and 'army of diversion,' but which terms the Emperor

1. See Appendix.

[59]

thought might lead to misconception on the part of our commanders. The Emperor made this observation in that very calm, quiet way, which has such a wonderful effect on every one. I sat watching his face and his peculiar eye while he was calculating the numbers on paper, which certainly are overwhelming, and I think *no* Russian army can withstand.

The good old Marshal, who understands and reads, though he cannot speak, English, was very plain and frank in everything he said, and helped to facilitate the discussion very much. I left them at twenty minutes past seven to dress for dinner; but they remained together, I think, for nearly twenty minutes longer.

We found the Emperor not quite ready when we went over to their apartments. The Empress looked particularly lovely in a white net dress *à deux jupes*, trimmed with scarlet velvet bows and bunches of white lilacs, and two bows of the same, and diamond flowers in her hair. She looked so simple and so elegant. I wish I could make a sketch of her as she was. I wore a blue dress, richly trimmed with lace, my rubies, and two feathers in my hair. The Emperor wore his General's uniform, shorts, a diamond garter and star; and Albert his very becoming Rifle uniform.[1] The children were as usual in the gallery to get a glimpse. As we were walking along, the Emperor told me, as a curious circumstance, that he has on *'les décorations de l'ordre de la Jarretière, qui appartiennent*

1. The Prince was Colonel-in-Chief of the Rifle Brigade. His portrait by Winterhalter in the uniform of the Brigade is in the National Portrait Gallery.

aux diamants de la Couronne, et qui ont été faites pour Charles X'. This is very extraordinary. In short, everything seems a dream. It was the star – a very large one – and the badge, not the garter, which, however, he had had made out of jewels belonging to the Crown.

We dined in the bow library, and we were seated as before, the Marshal next to me. He is so amusing, and really a charming old man. The Duchess of Wellington sat, both to-day and yesterday, next to the Emperor. We talked (the Emperor and I) of the council we had had, and I said I was convinced that, without the Emperor's presence here, we should not have come to an agreement of this importance. He repeated his intention of going to the Crimea, and said he only waited for decisive news from Vienna. I repeated my fear of his departure, the alarm it would cause, and begged he would not unnecessarily expose himself, which, he said, he certainly would not. '*Ah! mon Dieu,*' he said, '*si nous avions seulement un petit Prince Arthur!*' '*Mais, Sire, un petit enfant ne peut pas remplacer votre Majesté,*' was my reply. '*C'est vrai,*' he said, '*mais cela fait beaucoup dans l'imagination*'. I ventured, I said, to ask him if he found '*un appui*' in his cousin, Prince Napoleon. '*Ah! mon Dieu, non, voilà le malheur;*' that he was very clever, made himself appear much worse than he was; but that, he said, '*tout ce qui lui passe par la tête, il raisonne sur tout,*' and had made himself very unpopular with the army. '*Il a une activité sans but.*' He alluded to his family, which, for various reasons, from their dispersion, connections, &c., he had divided into '*famille impériale et civile*'. '*Au fond je*

ne sais pas trop ce que cela veut dire,' he said. The letters
or rather more correspondence of *le roi Joseph*[1] with
Napoleon, which Albert is reading, he regrets should
have been published; his uncle Jérôme never having
looked over them, because there were things in them,
orders, &c., '*qu'un gouvernement n'avoue pas*'.

The Emperor's love for England is very great.
'*L'Angleterre, c'est admirable; il faut me contenir devant
les Français;*' but that there was such a difference: '*il
y a une telle présomption,*' which is very true; that their
revolution had come later than ours, and yet that they
were a hundred years behind us. He regretted, and
was surprised, we did not increase our regular army.
I explained our difficulties; he complained of the slow-
ness in the English Government in giving answers to
proposals. I showed that this resulted necessarily from
the responsibility of Government to Parliament.

We went upstairs after dinner to the White drawing-room, where the Royal family, including Mama,
Vicky (in a point lace dress over pink), and the
Cambridges, and the Maharajah (Dhuleep Singh)
joined us; and we were soon followed by the Emperor
and Albert. The Walewskis had dined with us.

We went into the saloon for one of our usual
concerts: about four hundred people invited. I sat between the Emperor and the Empress. It was a good
concert. Between the acts (the Emperor leading me,
and Albert the Empress) we went first into the next
room, where we stood, and every one passed by, and

1. Elder brother of Napoleon I, who in 1806 became King of
Naples and from 1808 to 1813 was King of Spain.

we named them to the Emperor and Empress. He recognised all his old friends by shaking hands with them, and saying how glad he was to see them. Sir Edwin Landseer was amongst them. Then we went into the supper-room, and after staying there a little and talking to a few people, we went back to the concert-room for the short second act. When the *Préfet de la Seine*[1] was presented to me, he made a speech, hoping I would come to Paris, and, if I did, to the Hôtel de Ville. I could only answer by turning to the Emperor, and saying, I should be delighted to come to Paris some day. The Emperor was much annoyed by it and told me, '*J'en étais confondu; ils sont si bêtes en France, toujours des phrases*'.

During the concert the Emperor conversed on several important subjects with me, and he was altogether in so *causant* a mood, that I think he would have been inclined to converse upon many more delicate subjects even, upon which I certainly would have been glad to hear his own reasons, had there been any more time. Speaking of M. V. de Weyer,[2] who is a great and old friend of his, and for whom he has a sincere regard, he said, he could not understand how he (V. de W.) could have imagined that he meant to take possession of Belgium; that also '*on croyait que je voulais attaquer l'Angleterre, mais, mon Dieu! comment pouvait-on y croire? Il n'y avait pas le moindre prétexte!*' I answered that certainly people had had this idea, and

1. Baron Georges Haussmann, under whose aegis large areas of Paris were replanned and rebuilt during the Second Empire.
2. M. Sylvain van de Weyer, Belgian Foreign Minister.

that in England people certainly had sometimes very extraordinary notions, which they believed with the greatest pertinacity. In 1838, when he was staying at Beaudesert, Lady Anglesey told him 'que le roi Louis-Philippe voulait faire une descente sur l'Angleterre,' that he had told her, 'C'est absurde,' but she had still maintained it. The Emperor spoke to me also of M. Persigny[1], who was his faithful friend and follower, but who was so imprudent and so extravagant, that he did a great deal of harm in attributing opinions to him which did not exist.

All over by a quarter-past twelve. As we were taking them to their apartments, the Emperor said, how grieved he was that this was the last evening; that the time had passed so quickly. The Empress was quite low and sad.

Saturday, April 21st

We breakfasted for the last time with the Emperor (who, as well as every one else, was in uniform), and the war and the Vienna negotiations were talked of. He is evidently very anxious about the whole affair. *'J'ai bien peur des nouvelles de Vienne.'* He feared that our Ministers (Drouyn de Lhuys and Lord John[2]) would do something imprudent. *'Je n'ose pas le dire*

1. Le Comte de Persigny succeeded Count Walewski as French Ambassador later in 1855.
2. M. Edourd Drouyn de Lhuys, a member of the French Cabinet, and Lord John Russell, then Colonial Secretary, represented their respective governments in unsuccessful negotiations in Vienna for ending the Crimean War.

haut, mais j'avoue que j'ai peur qu'on ne fasse la paix avant qu'on ait pris Sébastopol, et qu'alors les deux armées se trouveront dans une position bien fâcheuse.' I feel this too. He then added, that he thought that he might come after preliminaries for peace were signed, go on with the siege, and possibly take the town. Albert very properly observed, that this would be very dangerous, and might have the appearance of *'manque de bonne foi'.* The Emperor paused, smiled, and then answered: *'Je ne peux rien répondre.'*

We went over to the Emperor's and Empress's apartments at a little before ten, with Mama, who had joined us, and all the children, and George (who was going down to Dover), and we remained there together with the Empress for some little time. The Emperor was not quite ready, and was delayed by writing into my autograph book, as well as in Bertie's and Vicky's. At near half-past ten we accompanied them downstairs. The Emperor, in returning me my album, said: *'J'ai tâché d'écrire ce que je sens.'* The words are: *'Je porte à votre Majesté les sentiments qu'on éprouve pour une reine et pour une sœur, dévouement respectueux tendre amitié –* NAPOLEON.*'*

As we were going along, the Emperor said, how much he had felt our kindness; what a *'bon souvenir'* they would carry back, and *'n'est-ce pas, vous viendrez à Paris cet été, si vous pouvez?'* I replied, Certainly, provided my public duties did not prevent me, which he quite understood. *'Je crois que d'avoir passé mon jour de naissance avec votre Majesté me portera bonheur, et le petit crayon que vous m'avez donné.'*

[65]   E

At the door there was quite a tender leave-taking. All our children, who had accompanied us, began to cry; the dear Empress also, saying she hoped she would see me soon again at Paris. '*Sans cela ce serait trop pénible de se séparer.*' She pressed my hand and embraced me three times. The Emperor kissed my hand twice, and I embraced him twice. The ladies and gentlemen and our ladies began to be *émues*, and I was very near being set off.

Away they drove, the band playing *Partant pour la Syrie* (which we had heard fourteen times on Thursday), and we ran up to see them drive away from the very saloon in which we had been together with them. The Emperor and Empress saw us at the window, turned round, got up and bowed. Albert and George were in the carriage with them. We watched them with the glittering escort till they could be seen no more, and then returned to our rooms. And thus this visit, this great event, has passed, as, alas! everything does in this world. It is a dream – a brilliant, successful, and pleasant dream, the recollection of which is firmly fixed in my mind. On all it has left a pleasant, satisfactory impression. It went off so beautifully, not a hitch nor *contretemps*, fine weather, everything smiling. The nation enthusiastic, and happy in the firm and intimate alliance and union of two great countries, whose enmity would prevent peace for their country. We have war now certainly, but war which does not threaten our shores, our homes, and internal prosperity, which war with France ever must do.

This visit was in many respects so peculiar, and

showed so strongly what the force of circumstances and what the lapse of time will do, that it forms one of the most curious pages of history. It is for that reason that I have been so minute in detailing everything. The impression it has left has been very pleasant, and I am very glad to know this wonderful and extraordinary man, whom it is certainly impossible not to like when you live with him, and not, to a great extent, to admire. We were ten hours together yesterday.

Many of his former acts seem incomprehensible, indeed many are seemingly inexcusable, and yet I believe him full of kindness, affection, friendship, and gratitude. I feel confidence in him as regards the future. I think he is frank, means well towards us. Stockmar[1] is delighted at the visit and our behaviour.

Could do nothing but talk of these great events, which, as usual with me, I am very sorry are past. I enjoyed everything so much. I had a short walk with Charles. The children were all quite melancholy, and so was I, everything seemed so dull. After luncheon we walked through the rooms, which are so pretty.

Albert returned at five, the Emperor and Empress having embarked at half-past one, and sailed with a favourable wind. He felt just as I did, much pleased with everything, liking the Emperor and Empress (the latter particularly), and being very much interested in them, and feeling quite excited and *'leer'* (empty), as I did. We could only talk, not do anything.

1. Baron Stockmar, tutor to Prince Albert. After the Prince's marriage he became his confidant and unofficial adviser.

SATURDAY, APRIL 21st

The Emperor wrote the following peculiar and very pretty lines in Bertie's book, which had been originally written for himself:

> *Jüngling mit der reinen Seele,*
> *Mit der Unschuld freiem Gefühle,*
> *Prüf' und wähle,*
> *Aber Lob sei nie dein Ziel!*
> *Ob Dir Beifall jauchzt die Menge,*
> *Ob sie lästert, wanke nicht.*
> *Trüglich oft sind Preisgesänge,*
> *Doch der Wahrheit Pfad ist enge,*
> *Zwischen Klüften geht die Pflicht.*

TRANSLATION:

> *Youth, of soul unstain'd and pure,*
> *Innocent and fresh in feeling,*
> *Choose and ponder, but be sure,*
> *World's praise never sways thy dealing!*
> *Though the crowd with plaudits hail thee,*
> *Though their calumnies assail thee,*
> *Swerve not; but remember, youth,*
> *Minstrel praises oft betray;*
> *Narrow is the path of Truth,*
> *Midst pitfalls lies Duty's way.*

I am sure this is what he feels himself, and believes himself to have done and be doing.

A late walk with Charles in the garden, and heard on returning by telegraph that the Emperor and Empress had landed safely at Boulogne at four. Saw Jane Ely, who had gone to Dover also, and said they were so pleased, that they felt our kindness so much, felt so much our allowing the children to associate with them, our treating them as equals, and that it would be everything for the Empress. The suite are also quite delighted. The gentlemen (ours) and Jane Ely, M. Seymour, and the two Maids of Honour, have all got fine presents. The Emperor has been very generous everywhere.

In all my descriptions I have omitted mentioning that the Emperor is an abstemious man, eating and drinking moderately, taking coffee and bread and butter only for breakfast, and a cup of coffee after dinner, and tea later in the evening.

We dined with our own people only; what we talked about is easily guessed.

May 2nd

The great advantage to be derived from the permanent alliance of England and France, which is of such vital importance to both countries, from the Emperor's recent visit, I take to be this: that with his peculiar character and views, which are very personal, a kind, unaffected, and hearty reception by us personally in our own family will make a lasting impression on his mind. He will see that he can rely upon our friendship and honesty towards him and his country, so long as he remains faithful towards us. Naturally frank, he will see the advantage to be derived from continuing so; and if he reflects upon the downfall of the former dynasty, he will see that it arose chiefly from a breach of pledges and ambiguous conduct towards this country and its sovereign, and will be sure, if I be not very much mistaken in his character, to avoid such a course.

It must likewise not be overlooked that this kindly feeling towards us, and consequently towards England (the interests of which are inseparable from us), must be increased when it is remembered that we are almost the only people in his own position with whom he has been able to be on terms of intimacy, consequently almost the only ones to whom he could talk easily and unreservedly . . . It is, therefore, natural to believe that he will not willingly separate from those who, like us, do not scruple to put him in possession of the real facts, and whose conduct is guided by justice and honesty . . . I would go still further: I think that it is in our power to keep him in the right course . . . We should never lose the opportunity of checking in the bud any attempt on the part of his agents or ministers to play us false, frankly informing him of the facts, and encouraging him to bring forward in an equally frank manner whatever he has to complain of. This is the course which we have hitherto pursued, and, as he is France in his sole person, it becomes of the utmost importance to encourage by every means in our power that very open intercourse which I must say has existed between him and Lord Cowley for the last year and a half, and now, since our personal intercourse, with ourselves . . .

THE VISIT OF THE QUEEN
AND H.R.H. THE PRINCE CONSORT
TO THE EMPEROR OF
THE FRENCH

Saturday, August 18*th,* 1855

Could not sleep for a long time for the heat, though the yacht is most comfortable. At five we got under way. From the rapidity with which the yacht goes, there is a great deal of vibration; and they were noisy on deck. After seven we got up: the day quite splendid, the sea deep blue, and quite smooth. At eleven we took the rest of the party on board. At one we were so close to Boulogne that we had to go round and round in order not to be too soon for the tide. At length, at twenty minutes past one, we steamed slowly into Boulogne, amidst the cheers of numbers of people on the pier, which was lined with troops *'qui battaient aux champs'*.

The scene was very brilliant. On the shore was the Emperor, surrounded by his officers, including the Maréchal Baraguay d'Hilliers, who commands the troops there, Lord Cowley, a regiment of Lancers, many horses, many people, the brilliant carriages, the troops covering the *Falaise* and constantly firing (musketry fire). All this, with a brilliant but broiling sun, had the gayest effect possible. There were 40,000 troops out! A *vivandière* stood close opposite to us, and was very conspicuous – while the yacht was being

[73]

brought up alongside the quay, which was a long and slow process, the Emperor standing there the whole time, and the troops constantly presenting arms! At length the bridge or gangway was adjusted, the Emperor stepped across, and I met him half way and embraced him twice; after which he led me on shore amidst acclamations, salutes, and every sound of joy and respect.

We four entered a landau carriage with glass windows and drove through the densely crowded and decorated streets, the Emperor escorting us himself on horseback. There was a tremendous crowd at the railroad (*la Gare*), and countless ladies. We got into a saloon with the Emperor, who was all kindness and civility. The heat on the railroad was very great, as was also the dust – really dreadful. I never felt hotter, but fortunately I had lost my headache.

The country for some distance is nothing particular – downs and flat country intersected with rows of poplars. We passed by different stations, Pont-Rémy, Fontaine, &c. At Abbeville, a large town with fortifications, we stopped. The authorities were waiting our arrival, with the *Garde Nationale*, and a regiment of dragoons. A very fat *Préfet* gave me an address. I admire the troops very much. They all shout: '*Vive la Reine d'Angleterre!*' '*Vive l'Empereur!*' '*Vive le Prince Albert!*' We reached Amiens at a quarter-past four. The *Gare* was handsomely decorated, the crowd immense – *Garde Nationale*, troops, authorities, the bishops, &c., many ladies, and all most enthusiastic. We got out a moment and received a nosegay.

[74]

At half-past four we started again. The country became prettier; many trees, valleys, rivers, small villages, and the fields divided into small partitions. The sun got lower, and the Emperor became very anxious we should arrive at Paris. We next came to Clermont, where the Mayor recognised Albert from former times. The day seemed fast closing, and our impatience to arrive increased. At length we passed St Leu, Montmorency, both charmingly situated; then got a glimpse of Montmartre, my first sight of Paris. We next came to Enghien, a small place near a lake, with many pretty villas; and at last we passed the fortifications, and Paris opened upon us.

Numbers of people about. Houses, people, everything so different from England, and so gay and lively. We at length entered the *Gare du chemin de fer de Strasbourg*, which was lit up and beautifully decorated, lined with troops, and filled with people. Prince Napoleon was there, and Maréchal Magnan,[1] the Général Lowestine commanding the *Garde Nationale*. We proceeded at once to the carriages, which were drawn up at a point where the *coup-d'œil* was truly magnificent. We entered a carriage with four horses, Vicky and I sitting together (it seemed to me a dream that she should appear *comme une grande personne*), the Emperor and Albert opposite – of course all in uniform. Unfortunately I have so little time to write, that I cannot attempt any description in detail. One impression is succeeded by another. But, indeed, no description can give an idea of the splendour of the

1. He had assisted Napoleon III in the *coup d'état* of 1851.

whole scene. Paris is the most beautiful and the gayest of cities, with its high handsome houses, in every one of which there is a shop. Imagine all these decorated in the most tasteful manner possible, with banners, flags, arches, flowers, inscriptions, and finally illuminations; the windows full of people up to the tops of the houses, which tower up storey upon storey, the streets lined with troops – National Guards and troops of the Line (with the *Chasseurs d'Afrique*) – beautifully kept, and everybody most enthusiastic; and yet you will have but a faint notion of this triumph as it was.

There were endless cries of '*Vive la Reine d'Angleterre!*' '*Vive l'Empereur!*' '*Vive le Prince Albert!*' The approaching twilight rather added to the beauty of it all, and it was still quite light enough, when we passed down the new Boulevard de Strasbourg (the Emperor's creation) – the Boulevards – by the Porte St Denis, la Madeleine, the Place de la Concorde, and the Arc de Triomphe, de l'Etoile, all splendid structures. By the time we reached the Place de la Concorde it unfortunately became very dark, and we could hardly distinguish the Champs Elysées and Bois de Boulogne. There were troops along the whole line from the *Gare* to the Palace, who '*battaient aux champs,*' and bands playing *God Save the Queen*. There were 40,000 troops, besides the 20,000 National Guards – 60,000 in all; besides the 40,000 I saw at Boulogne: artillery, cavalry, *Cent-Gardes* (who are splendid), and last, but not least, to my great delight, at the Bridge of Boulogne, near the village and Palace of St-Cloud,[1] the Zouaves – splendid troops in splendid dress, the friends of my dear Guards!

In all this blaze of light from lamps, torches, amidst the roar of cannon, and bands, and drums, and cheers, we reached the Palace. The dear Empress, with Princess Mathilde[2] and the ladies, received us at the door, and took us up a beautiful staircase, lined by the splendid *Cent-Gardes*, who are magnificent men, very like our Life-Guards, and with helmets, cuirasses, a light blue uniform and crimson facings, and carry a musket with a sword fixed at the top.

We went at once to our rooms, which are charming, and of which more hereafter. I felt quite bewildered, but enchanted. It was like a fairy tale, and everything so beautiful! Many of our things had not come: and two of my ladies could not appear.[3] The Marquis de la Grange, the Comte de Belmont, the Vicomte Walsh, Colonel Fleury, Madame Labédoyère, and Madame de Rayneval are attached to us. The

1. Burnt by the Prussians in 1871.
2. Daughter of Jérôme, King of Westphalia and sister of Prince Napoleon.
3. The suite who accompanied the Queen and Prince to France consisted of: The Marchioness of Ely, Lady Churchill (Ladies-in-Waiting), the Hon. Mary Bulteel (Maid of Honour), the Marquis of Breadalbane (Lord Chamberlain), the Earl of Clarendon (Secretary for Foreign Affairs), the Marquis of Abercorn (Groom of the Stole to the Prince), Lord Alfred Paget (Clerk Marshal,) General the Hon. C. Grey (Equerry-in-Waiting and Secretary to the Prince), Colonel the Hon. C. Phipps (Privy Purse), Colonel Biddulph (Master of the Household), Sir J. Clark (Physician to the Queen), Miss Hildyard (Governess to the Princess Royal), and Mr Gibbs (tutor to the Prince of Wales).

Emperor came to fetch us. The Empress did not dine, being very tired; but the Princesse d'Essling, and another lady, Madame de Saulecy, the *Grandes Charges*, aides-de-camp, Comte Walewski, and M. Fould[1] (not pleasing looking), dined. Also Princess Mathilde. She was very civil.

The saloons are splendid, all *en suite*, and, as well as the court-yard, staircase, &c., remind me of Brühl. The ceilings are beautifully painted, and the walls hung with Gobelins. One or two busts of the Imperial family, Napoleon, his parents, &c., are there. The Salle-de-Mars is a very fine room, and opens into the fine long gallery called La Salle-de-Diane, in which we dined. The room was overpoweringly hot, for the table was covered with lights, which quite dazzled one: everything magnificent, but all very quiet, very different from things in the poor King's time – much more royal.

The Emperor (of course) led me in, and I sat between him and Albert, who led in Princesse Mathilde. Maréchal Magnan and Général Lowestine (a *ci-devant jeune homme* of seventy) also dined with us. Everybody so civil and kind. The night was beautiful when we stepped out on the balcony. Maréchal Magnan told me, that such enthusiasm as we had witnessed had not been known in Paris – not in the time of the Emperor Napoleon's triumphs; and Général Lowestine said that all France would have come, if there had been time. The National Guard were particularly civil and

1. M. Achille Fould, a Jewish banker, and Minister in the French government.

friendly; all regretted our arriving so late. At length at twelve we got to rest.

St-Cloud, Sunday, August 19th

Slept very well, and awoke to admire our lovely room. We have a number of rooms *en suite*, furnished with the greatest taste; the walls of most of them white and gold; and the ceilings of my sitting and drawing rooms painted to represent sky. My rooms are a bedroom, and then a little bath-room and dressing-room – looking on Paris (the view of which is splendid); a sitting-room and drawing-room (quite lovely), and two more rooms – all looking out on the garden, with its fountains and beautiful long avenues of beech-trees, with orange-trees, and fine and very beautiful flowers. These regular old gardens are beautiful and very gay. Albert's suite of rooms joins on from our bedroom and looks into the court-yard. They have all been freshly decorated and *meublées*. A balcony goes all round, and the windows have outside shutters, as in all *châteaux* abroad. The court-yard, too, is so pretty.

While dressing, I stopped to look at the *Cent-Gardes*, very like our Life Guards – magnificent men of six feet and upwards – riding by; and then hearing a charming sort of *fanfare*, I ran to another window, and saw a body of Zouaves marching up, preceded by buglers. They look so handsome, and walk so lightly.

At nine we breakfasted with the children, and the

Emperor, who had kindly come to fetch us, in a fine large room, on the other side of the staircase, very handsomely furnished with green, and the ceiling and cornices splendidly gilt in three different colours of gold. Excellent coffee, and charming china and plate, and all so quietly served. The Emperor was very kind and amiable and quiet, and he seems to be in excellent spirits.

After breakfast he proposed we should take a little drive in the Park, and we walked out of the next room door, which is *au rez-de-chausée*, the Palace being built against a high hill. The garden next the Orangery is beautiful, and planted with the most brilliant flowers. There are rows of orange-trees. Our carriages were two phaetons with bay ponies. The Emperor drove me himself, and Albert and the two children followed in the next carriage. We drove along and round about the Park, which is beautiful; along numberless shady avenues, with beautiful foliage, and charming glimpses of country. All that part is private. We passed Villeneuve-l'Etang, a little villa which the Emperor has bought, surrounded by its own grounds and park, which he tries to make as English and as private as possible, longing to get away from etiquette and restraint. We stopped at the guard-house of the Zouaves, and spoke to one who had been in the Crimea, and then drove along the beautiful terrace. The Emperor was most amiable and kind, and talked of all sorts of things. He is much pleased at the good news from the Crimea. The Russians have lost enormously, about 5,000 men.

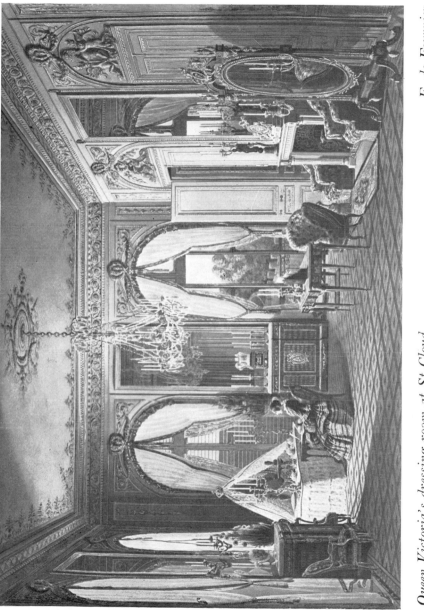

Queen Victoria's dressing-room at St-Cloud

F. de Fournier

The Tableau of the Allies, represented by Prince Arthur, Princess Louise and Princess Helena. Photograph by Bambridge.

At half-past eleven prayers were read by the Chaplain of the Embassy, in the room next to where we breakfasted. Visited Vicky's and Bertie's charming rooms just below, hung with beautiful little pictures, and opening on a lovely little flower-garden. You had to pass a small hall, in which the *Cent-Gardes* wait: they are splendid men, and their dress very handsome. Two always stand at the top of the staircases. The dear Empress lunched with us, and looked so pretty in a white barége dress over white, made like a sort of *peignoir*. After the luncheon they left us, and I dressed and rested, though but little, for there is always so much going on.

At five we drove out in a barouche (as we always do) with the Empress and Emperor, the children and ladies and gentlemen following, and drove about in the Bois de Boulogne, which is beautiful, and which the Emperor has made especially so by a piece of artificial water, and cascades, and new drives. Albert is quite astonished at it, and says it is simply wonderful to see the improvements which have been made. Hearing me express a wish to know where Neuilly was, both the Emperor and Empress very amiably proposed to take us there. We accordingly drove there, going by several pretty country houses, through the very small dirty little village of Neuilly, into the gates, where we found two pavilions, all in ruins, with broken windows, grass growing in the walks, presenting altogether a most melancholy picture of destruction and neglect. Albert remembered the place so well. We returned by the banks of the

Seine, which are very picturesque and remind one of Richmond. The rows of poplars and houses with their coloured shutters are so pretty and gay. A great many people cheering everywhere; many driving under the trees in the Bois de Boulogne. The village of St-Cloud – the gayest thing in the world – lined with people, soldiers, Zouaves, *Gardes Impériales*, &c. &c. The river is just below St-Cloud, with trees down to the banks. Its effect in the landscape is beautiful.

A large dinner-party, but not many invitations. General Canrobert,[1] only just returned from the trenches – *'j'étais dans les tranchées il y a quinze jours'* – was the principal addition. He sat next to me, and I was delighted with him, such an honest good man, so sincere and friendly, and *so* fond of the English, very enthusiastic, talking with much gesticulation. He is short, and wears his hair, which is black, rather long behind, has a red face and rolling eyes, moustaches, and no whiskers, and carries his head rather high. He praised our troops immensely, spoke of the great difficulty of the undertaking, the sufferings we had all undergone, the mistakes which had been made, and so kindly of our generals and troops. I said I looked upon him as an old acquaintance, from having heard so much of him. He said, *'Je suis presque un sujet de votre Majesté,'* from being a member of the Fishmongers'. Speaking of poor Lord Raglan[2] he said, *'C'était un noble gentleman, que nous avons beaucoup*

1. Commander-in-Chief of the French forces in the Crimea.
2. Former Commander-in-Chief of the British forces in the Crimea, who had died there in June.

regretté;' and of the 18th (the unsuccessful attack on the Redan and the Malakoff), *'Cela a tué le pauvre Milord.'*

The dear Empress, who sat opposite with Albert, had a white *organdi* dress, embroidered with blue and straw, with turquoise and diamond ornaments, and I a green silk dress, trimmed with lace, and roses and violets in my hair. Vicky and Bertie appeared after dinner.

We separated at a quarter to eleven. The windows all open, and the evening beautiful. I sat next the dear Empress, the gentlemen all standing. I forgot to mention that after luncheon, the Emperor presented all his Ministers to me. M. Fould, who is in fact the Prime Minister,[1] and Walewski, were at the door when we arrived.

Monday, August 20th – St-Cloud

A lovely morning, pleasant air, with a bright sun, and the delicious fountains playing. Further satisfactory accounts from the Crimea. The Russians have lost more than 3,000 men. The French have buried some and the Russians others.

The Emperor came to fetch us for breakfast, as before. The coffee quite excellent, and all the cookery very plain and very good. For breakfast and luncheon we have a small round table as at home. Lovely Sèvres china, beautiful plate, some old plate, *qui date*

1. This was presumably a slip of the pen: M. Fould was Minister of State.

de l'Empire, but on which *fleur-de-lis* had been placed. The servants very quiet and attentive.

At a quarter-past ten, we started for Paris with all our suite. The Emperor has pretty barouches, rather smaller than ours, and bay horses, harnessed quite as ours are, the livery dark green, black and gold, with red and gold waistcoats. We drove by the Bois de Boulogne, the new Avenue de l'Impératrice, which is being planted and will be very fine, through that splendid Arc de Triomphe, which was finished in Louis-Philippe's time, along the Champs-Elysées (our usual road every day) to the *Exposition des Beaux-Arts*, which is in it, and which is connected with the *Palais de l'Industrie*. Prince Napoleon, M. Fould (*Ministre d'Etat*), and a number of gentlemen connected with the Exhibition, M. Delblaye being the principal one, and all the foreign Commissioners, received us.

All the different schools are represented, French, English, German, Italian, Spanish, Belgian, &c., and there are some very fine things, many, of course, not new works, for they have collected those of all the different masters. H. Vernet's are very fine. We were nearly squeezed in one of the large rooms, the public having been unfortunately let in, but, after that, they were excluded from each room into which we went.

The enthusiasm was very great, both there and in the densely crowded streets and cries of '*Vive l'Empereur!*' '*Vive la Reine d'Angleterre!*' were very constant and gratifying. I was, of course, always at the Emperor's arm. The children were with us. (In the

[84]

carriage, Vicky sits next to me, and Bertie goes in the second carriage.) There is a sculpture gallery, and upstairs, drawings, &c. The heat was intense. Prince Napoleon not very gracious. Winterhalter's large picture of the Empress and her ladies is very fine.

We drove from here to the Elysée in town carriages – ours being very handsome, lined with white satin and gold. We have always an escort, either *Cent-Gardes*, or *Cuirassiers de la Garde*. The Elysée is very pretty, but not neatly fitted up – except one or two rooms – and is small. Here again were rooms prepared for us; and there were many souvenirs of Napoleon in the Emperor's rooms (which we had), *'la Reine Hortense'*,[1] &c. There we took luncheon with the Emperor (we five, I mean, together as always), in a room where the portraits of all the Sovereigns our contemporaries are.

This quiet luncheon over, Albert went up to put on his uniform, and the Emperor kindly took Bertie out in his curricle, which he drove himself – one with two servants behind – not the least interesting incident in this most eventful, interesting, and delightful visit – and drove him about Paris. We then saw Prince Adalbert of Bavaria,[2] of whom more hereafter; next the gentlemen attached to the British Embassy; and lastly the whole *corps diplomatique*, with their wives, and who were assembled in a room, and presented to

1. Queen of Holland and mother of Napoleon III. She was a daughter of the Empress Josephine by her first marriage to the Comte de Beauharnais.
2. Youngest son of Leopold I, King of Bavaria.

me by Lord and Lady Cowley. This over, the Emperor took us round the very shady pretty little garden, and we re-entered the open carriages and drove across the Place de la Concorde, most magnificent, where poor Louis XVI, Marie-Antoinette, and so many others were guillotined; thence along the beautiful Boulevards, the Rue de Rivoli, which is quite new, the Emperor having cleared away numberless old streets and replaced them by this great new magnificent line of street, past the new part of the Louvre, the design of which is truly splendid; then by the Pont-au-Change, facing the Hôtel de Ville – on to the Palais de Justice, from the steps of which the view of the richly decorated streets and of the enthusiastic thousands assembled was splendid. We then visited the Sainte-Chapelle, which adjoins the Palais de Justice, and has been most exquisitely restored. It is small, and of the purest early Gothic, and is celebrated for containing the heart of St Louis, by whom it was built. In passing the neighbouring bridge, where you have a very fine view of the town, you see the Conciergerie, and the Emperor, pointing to it, said: *'Voilà où j'étais en prison.'* Strange, incredible contrast, to be driving with us as Emperor through the streets of the town in triumph!

We next went to Notre-Dame. The outside is magnificent, but the inside has nothing to admire, except the carving of the choir. The Emperor was married there. The Archbishop of Paris and the clergy received us. We next went to the Hôtel de Ville, which is magnificent, and the street leading to which

is now being made – the whole having been opened
out. We then proceeded by the Boulevards, passing
the Place de la Bastille, where the Colonne de Juillet
is placed, the Fontaine du Château d'Eau, the Porte
St Martin and Porte St Denis, and thence along the
Rue de la Paix, the Rue Castiglione, full of beautiful
shops and houses, the Place Vendôme, where Napoleon's statue is, and then home the usual way, reach-
ing St-Cloud by nearly six o'clock. Everything so gay,
so bright – very hot, but the air so light and so very
clear that everything stands out clear and sharp
against the horizon. The absence of smoke helps to
make everything white and bright, and this in Paris,
with the quantity of gilding about the shops, green
shutters, &c., produces a brilliancy of effect that is
quite indescribable. The decoration of the streets
generally is most beautiful.

We visited the dear Empress, who received us upstairs, for a short while, and then went to our rooms.
No one can be kinder or more agreeable than the
Emperor, and he is so quiet, which is such a comfort
on all occasions, but particularly on such as these. The
view of Paris from our rooms and balcony, with a
charming little garden just below my dressing-room
window, lit up by the evening light, the Arc de
Triomphe rising beautifully and conspicuously in the
distance, had a marvellous effect. I sat drawing on the
balcony, and took a little sketch of the avenue looking
down into the town of St-Cloud, all so pretty.

Afterwards, on going to Albert's room, I found
Canrobert with him, who told us much that was very

interesting – in fact, quite touching – about his own position and his feeling towards Lord Raglan, the record of which I shall defer to another time. I gave him the Order of the Bath, and with real pleasure. I was obliged to give it also, but *à contre-cœur*, before dinner, to Prince Napoleon, whose manner is rude and disagreeable in the highest degree. *Il me fait peur*, and has a diabolical expression.

Dinner at eight, of between seventy and eighty people. Prince Napoleon and Princesse Mathilde were of the party. The dear Empress had on a dress embroidered with cornflowers, and a sapphire and diamond diadem. I had a pink dress, with opals and diamonds, and my diadem. I sat between the Emperor and Prince Napoleon. The Emperor showed us the Crown jewels, or rather the Imperial crowns, which he has had freshly mounted, and in one of which, the Regent, is a splendid stone. The crowns themselves, however, he had had made with very few diamonds, and used them for *parures* of the Empress.

After *cercleing* a little, we went to the theatre, going through the fine rooms, and along the celebrated Orangerie, in which the Convention sat, and out of which they were driven *le* 10 *Brumaire* [*sic*]. The theatre is small, but extremely pretty, and was full of company. I sat between the Emperor and Empress; next the Emperor, Vicky, whom Prince Napoleon had led, then Prince Adalbert of Bavaria, a very singular person, and next the Empress, Albert, the Princesse Mathilde, and Bertie. In the front row, adjoining the Imperial seats, were the Comtesse Montijo and the

Duchesse d'Albe, the Empress's mother and sister. The performance was *Les Demoiselles de St-Cyr*,[1] in which Regnier and Mademoiselle Brohan acted extremely well; the *ensemble* was perfect.

After the theatre we returned to the rooms upstairs, and stopped in the Salle-de-Mars, where everybody passed by, the Empress presenting each. We afterwards went for a moment into la Salle-de-Diane, where the refreshments were, the same in which we dined, and then went to our rooms, to which the Emperor and Empress, preceded by their gentlemen, always take us. It was near one. The night was delightfully warm, and we stepped out on the balcony to watch the carriages departing. We receive telegraphic accounts of the children every evening.

Tuesday, *August 21st*

Had not slept well, feeling too excited to get to sleep. (I write this from Osborne, August 28, where we landed safely at half-past ten, having arrived at half-past eight after an excellent passage, and feel quite bewildered at the change, and sad.) After breakfasting, as usual, with the Emperor, quietly and comfortably, at about half-past nine, we got up and returned to our rooms, the Emperor leading me. The Zouaves were replaced by the *Garde Impériale*, very fine, and who are dressed very much like Napoleon's Guard, without the gaiters, and white leather

1. By Alexandre Dumas, *père*.

breeches. We were much grieved at poor Sir Arthur Torrens[1] being so dangerously ill; he had ridden in the cortège on our way into Paris. At half-past ten we started for Versailles in many carriages, *en poste*, the postilions in the old dress, but in the service of the Emperor himself.

We passed by Ville d'Avray, a pretty village, with many villas about it. It was decorated with wreaths, &c.; the people everywhere out and very friendly. We drove up a road, on each side of which were trees. This is the case with most of the roads. Everywhere almost where there was a village, were troops or National Guards, and always some *gendarmes* in their handsome dress. We reached Versailles in rather more than half an hour, and came in sight of the magnificent Palace, with its terraces, gardens, and fountains. It is enormous, with endless buildings attached to it, and of the greatest historic interest, reminding one of St-Simon at every step. We ascended the large staircase, and walked through all the large rooms and galleries. These are covered with historical pictures, some of the time, and many which poor King Louis-Philippe, whose great and most valuable work this was, had caused to be painted and placed where they now hang. These pictures record all Napoleon's battles and the events of his day, as well as of the Revolution, of the reigns of Louis XIV and Louis XV (many old and curious), and even of

1. British Military Commissioner in Paris, where he died a few days after this was written, as a result of wounds received in the Crimea.

more ancient times. Then again come pictures of the
events of poor Louis-Philippe's reign, of his sons'
campaigns in Africa, by Horace Vernet (of which
several of the finest are in the Exposition). Then
Louis XIV's rooms with portraits of the family; his
room and bed worked by the Demoiselles de St-Cyr,[1]
with the *ruelle*[2] before it; Louis XV's small apartments; Madame de Maintenon's, with her *Oratoire*;
rooms of poor Louis XVI and Marie-Antoinette, from
one of which she made her escape. All was most
interesting, instructive, and melancholy. There are
two statues on the staircase of Louis-Philippe and
Napoleon, and long outer galleries full of either
originals or casts of statues, and monuments of all the
sovereigns, princes, and people of note connected with
the history of France. The room with pictures representing the Crusades is very handsome, and quite in
accordance with the time depicted.

We went into the Chapel, where everything has
remained as in the time of Louis XIV, and which is
like our Chapel Royal, with a large pew, in which one
can well imagine Louis XIV present to hear mass.
I cannot enumerate the many other curious things,
rooms, &c., which we saw, as it would take too much
time. But they made a deep impression on me, and
seemed to bring back all the French history, with its
many strange and dark events, to our mind. And to

1. Young ladies of the school founded by Louis XIV and
Madame de Maintenon.
2. That part of the bedchamber reserved for courtiers attend-
ing the levée.

see all this with the Emperor was even more striking. It is a pleasure, however, to see how well everything has been preserved, and everything left by the Emperor in its place as he found it.

The view of the park and terraces from the windows is very fine. Vicky and Bertie were with us; Vicky, as usual, sitting next to me in the same carriage with the Emperor and ourselves. We drove about the very curious old-fashioned gardens, to see the waterworks, which are wonderful and endless. The effect of the innumerable *jets-d'eau* with the bright sunshine, bands playing (there were four in different parts of the gardens), the crowds of people and the numerous equipages going in and out of the small avenues and winding along the *bassins*, was very fine – quite magical.

We drove from here to the Grand-Trianon, another small palace, with rooms on the ground-floor, where Marie-Antoinette used to live, and from the windows of which there is a beautiful view. The Emperor showed me the room and bed (it had belonged to Napoleon), which had been prepared for us by poor Louis-Philippe when he expected us to visit Paris, and the sedan chair of Madame de Maintenon, next to which, according to St-Simon, Louis XIV used so often to walk; also the pretty little chapel (excessively small), in which poor Marie[1] was married to Alexander of Würtemberg in 1838. The garden is very pretty, and the Emperor picked me a flower to dry.

1. Second daughter of King Louis-Philippe.

We again got into the carriages and drove through the gardens, full of brilliant flowers, including a number of gladioli, which they put in large quantities into the gardens here, and which enliven the landscape very greatly, to the Petit-Trianon, that is to say, not to the small palace, but to the grounds. These are full of beautiful trees – many very rare ones – planted by poor Marie-Antoinette herself, and fine beeches and chestnuts of a great height, surrounded by pieces of water. Here there are different little cottages, all built by that poor unhappy queen, with different names: *le Curé, le Meunier, le Moulin,* &c., of which the Emperor takes great care, as indeed he does of all the palaces and historical records. In the largest of these buildings we lunched – we always alone with the Emperor, and (if she is there) the dear Empress. Here she joined us, and lunched with us. Everywhere, everything is ready, rooms prepared for us, and all just as if one were living there. The furniture (which I believe comes from the *Garde-Meuble*[1]) was frequently of that period of the Empire *'qui a un cachet tout particulier,'* and of which Mama had much at Kensington; so that in many places I recognised old acquaintances, in bureaux, mirrors, tables, presses, &c., also pendants to things which we have at Windsor in china, and in *meubles* of the time of Louis XIV, Louis XV and Louis XVI.

The Guides (that excellent band) played at and after luncheon, and after luncheon we sat for some

1. A warehouse for storing furniture and effects belonging to the State.

time under the fine trees, listening to the pretty music. Part of the time I sketched. The sun shining through the trees on this band, the ladies and gentlemen, the escort (*Carabiniers de la Garde*) and the postilions and horses, with the music and the occasional tinkling of the bells of the horses of the *chaises-de-poste*, produced the prettiest effect possible. At a little after three we started again for dear St-Cloud, which I doat [*sic*] on, I driving in a phaeton with the Empress, who had some cushions, or rather a bench, put into the carriage, which enabled her to lie down. Crowds all along the road; the sun intensely hot (I have never felt such heat, but at the same time never have a headache, the air being so light), and a great deal of dust, the country being so sandy. We went another way, by the Bois de Verrière, and came in by Villeneuve-l'Etang, at half-past four. Went to our delightful rooms, where the furniture is so charming and so well stuffed, that by lying a little while on the sofa you are completely rested.

Looked at prints and things of all kinds, which I am anxious to buy. The view on Paris this splendid evening again most beautiful. The air is so light and clear, and so devoid of our baneful coal smoke, that everything in the greatest distance is seen quite clearly and distinctly.

We dined (dressed) with the Emperor *à trois* in the same room in which we breakfast and lunch, at a quarter to seven; and at quarter-past seven we started with our large suite for Paris, the Emperor and Empress being with us; the gentlemen in uniform;

the Empress in a light white dress, with emerald and diamond diadem; and I, in white with coloured ribbons (which the Emperor admired very much) and also my emeralds and diamonds, including my diadem. (Curious to say, we found Princesse Mathilde also dressed in white, and with emeralds and diamonds, and a diadem.) Paris was brilliantly illuminated, and with the greatest taste. Under one of the triumphal arches was a lustre of lamps, which was extremely handsome. The streets were full of people cheering. The *Gardes de Paris* lined the staircase of the Grand Opéra, which is in the Rue Lepelletier, and at the top of the staircase in the vestibule were my favourite *Cent-Gardes.* Prince Napoleon and Princesse Mathilde met us there.

The box was arranged in the centre of the house, just as when we go to the Opera in state, two *Cent-Gardes* standing where the Yeomen stand, on either side of the box, and two also on the stage. The theatre is handsome and was full of people, and the reception very hearty. The heat was quite fearful, and the Empress was in a great state about it, and tried all she could to get *un peu d'air.* Count Bacciochi has the management of all the theatres, balls, concerts, &c. The first part of the performance was a selection of airs, duets, and trios from different operas, sung *en costume*, which I did not think a very happy arrangement. The second was the ballet of *La Touti*,[1] in three

1. In fact, it was called *La Fonti*, with music by Labarre and choreography by Mazilier. Possibly this mistake arose through a mis-reading of the Queen's handwriting.

acts, too long, though with fine decorations. Rosati was the principal performer. The scene then changed, and a view of Windsor, with the Emperor's arrival, appeared, and *God Save the Queen* was sung splendidly, and most enthusiastically cheered. There could not have been more enthusiasm in England.

We returned home at half-past twelve. The Empress was tired. The Emperor was very cheerful, and repeated with Albert all sorts of old German songs, and Albert repeated some to him. The Emperor is very fond of Germany and his old recollections, and there is much that is German in his character.

Wednesday, August 22nd

Another most splendid day. Most truly do the heavens favour and smile upon this happy alliance, for, when the Emperor was in England in April, the weather was beautiful. Despatches arrived (telegraphic, from General Simpson[1]), saying that they had begun a vertical fire, which was taking good effect. The Emperor is full of anxiety and regret about the campaign. Ten thousand shells have been thrown into the town within the last few days, and they are in want of more! At about a quarter to ten we started *en poste* for Paris (Vicky and Bertie with us). Always an escort too, which met us at the Bois de Boulogne,

1. General Sir James Simpson succeeded Lord Raglan as Commander-in-Chief in the Crimea after the latter's death in June 1855.

The Prince Napoleon. Photograph by Roger Fenton.

through which we always drove, passing under the Arc de l'Etoile [Triomphe], the proportions of which are truly magnificent, and along the Champs-Elysées.

We drove at once to the *Exposition*, where Prince Napoleon and all the gentlemen connected with the *Exposition* met us. The Emperor always leads me about everywhere. We walked generally through the nave, the *coup-d'œil* of which is very fine, looking at the different works of Art, and visiting the different exhibitions of the other countries. England and the Colonies make a very fine show, and our china pleases very much. We remained some time in the large court devoted to the *productions des manufactures royales*, which are *quite* magnificent: first of all the Crown jewels, which are truly superb, and most beautifully set, Sèvres porcelain most beautiful (I bought *one* small object), and a service of plate for the Emperor of the most splendid and tasteful design, beautiful furniture, and magnificent Gobelins and Beauvais tapestry. The Emperor kindly gave Albert a splendid vase of Sèvres manufacture, representing the Exhibition of 1851, which, he said, was particularly intended for Albert, as to *him* that Exhibition was due. Albert was much pleased, for it is a *chef-d'œuvre* in every sense of the word.

There are numbers of beautiful things in the Exhibition of all kinds, many which I recognise from the Exhibitions of London and Dublin. The machinery, which is very fine, we only glanced at, and we did not go upstairs at all.

At a little before two we drove to the Tuileries.[1] It is a very fine and truly royal palace, with a beautiful and very gay, though (except a very small enclosure in front of the palace) entirely public garden. The Emperor took us into his apartments, up a short flight of steps. They consist of a suite of rooms all opening one into the other, six in number, at the end of which is his bedroom and a small dressing-room; and they have been newly and handsomely done up. These he allowed us to use. In his bedroom are busts of his father and uncle, and an old glass case or bureau, which he had with him in England, and which contains all sorts of relics, that are peculiarly valuable to him.

In some of the other rooms are portraits of Napoleon, Joséphine, his own mother with his elder brother,[2] and one of her with his brother and himself as little children. These were in the room in which we lunched, and which is used as a sitting-room. There is also here the cabinet on which Louis-Philippe signed that fatal abdication. The Emperor took us upstairs by a small private staircase where the Empress's rooms are, into a room where I received the *Préfet* and the *Municipalité*, who came to invite us to the ball at the Hôtel de Ville, and wished to read an address, which the Emperor stopped. I answered that I would with pleasure go to the ball, that I had been deeply touched by the reception I had met with in France, and that I should never forget it. The *Préfet*

1. Burnt by the Commune in 1871. Only the Jardin des Tuileries now remains.
2. Napoleon Charles, who died in infancy in 1807.

then asked, whether they might call that new street leading to the Hôtel de Ville after me, which, I said, *'je serai bien flattée de cela, si l'Empereur le permet,'* turning towards him. He assented with pleasure; and I then observed upon the beauty of the town, and all that the Emperor had done for Paris.

This over, we went down to luncheon; Prince Napoleon joined us, and we were six. He was as usual contradictory and speaking of *'les ouvriers,'* whom he always tries to put forward. He seems to take pleasure in saying something disagreeable and biting, particularly to the Emperor, and with a smile which is quite satanic. The luncheon over, the Emperor left us, and we went upstairs with the children and ladies and gentlemen, and M. de Belmont,[1] to see the state rooms, which are magnificent: the Salle Blanche, Salle du Trône, Salle de la Paix, la Salle des Maréchaux, which is splendid, and beautifully redecorated by the Emperor, who has had to re-decorate the Tuileries entirely after the horrors of 1848; then the Galerie de Diane, a long room, which has to be divided, the Chapel (nothing very particular, and like ours in the Palaces), and the Theatre, which is very pretty. Everything is so truly regal, so large, so grand, so comprehensive; it makes me jealous that our great country, and particularly our great metropolis, should have nothing of the same kind to show! The view from the middle window of the Salle des Maréchaux, looking up the garden of the Tuileries to the Place de la Concorde, is very fine indeed. The Emperor thinks

1. M. le Comte de Belmont, attached to the Queen's suite.

the obelisk spoils the view. Where that very obelisk stands, Louis XVI, Marie-Antoinette, '*et tant d'autres furent guillotinés*'. What sad reflections does this not give rise to!

The Emperor met us as we were coming out of the theatre, and led us over the Pavillon Marsan, where Louis-Philippe and his family used to live, and which is miserable. He intends building a suite of apartments, in which to receive us, over the Orangery, or at least where the Orangery was. He left us to enable us to receive, first, M. and Mme Drouyn de Lhuys (he embarrassed, she much altered and grown very stout), and then the Princesse de Chimay.[1] After this, at half-past three, I went with Vicky and one of the French ladies, Lady Ely and two gentlemen, to the English Embassy in the Rue St-Honoré, in the Emperor's carriage. It is very pretty indeed, and newly furnished; the garden very much like that at the Elysée. Bertie had meantime gone out walking with Colonel Biddulph and M. Gibbs. Albert left me there to pay visits to Prince Napoleon, &c., and I went over the house with Lady Cowley, whose girls (pretty girls) were there. Drove back again and was met by the Emperor, who kindly wrote down, while I was in his room, the altered arrangements for Friday. Rested a little in the rooms (the Emperor's) allotted to us.

Albert returned from his visits, and we immediately started on our *incog.* drive, with considerable tribulation. The Emperor was much amused, and ordered

1. Wife of Prince de Chimay, personal agent of Leopold I of Belgium at the Court of Paris.

where we were to go. We got into a *remise*. I and
Mary Bulteel had provided ourselves with common
bonnets. I wore a black veil, down, and a black mantilla, and we sat together. Albert sat back, and Vicky,
who had also another bonnet and mantilla, which we
sent for in a hurry, did the same. We started. Just
as we were going through the gates the curious crowd
looked very much into the carriage, which was stopped
for a moment, and we felt very foolish. However, we
got away, and by help of my veil I was able to look
out, and we took a charming long drive by the Rue
de Rivoli, Rue Castiglione, where there are so many
fine shops, Place Vendôme, Rue de la Paix, all along
the Boulevards des Capucins, des Italiens, Montmartre, Poissonnière, Bonne-Nouvelle, St-Denis, St-
Martin, du Temple, des Filles du Calvaire, Beau-
marchais, by the Place de la Bastille, where stands the
Colonne de Juillet, the Boulevard Bourdon, Place
Mazas, thence across the Pont d'Austerlitz, with its
beautiful view up and down the river, and along the
quais, with everything so light, and white, and bright,
quantities of people and soldiers in bright colours,
marchands de coco, &c.; the people sitting and drinking
before the houses, all so foreign and southern-looking
to my eyes, and *so* gay. We then drove along the
Place de Wulhubert to the Jardin des Plantes, then
by the Marché aux Fleurs (very pretty along the
quai), Halle aux Vins (a number of curious little
houses in a sort of garden), Quai de la Tournelle,
Quai Montebello, Quai St-Michel, the Pont-au-
Change, opposite the old Tower of St-Jacques, Quai

[101]

de la Mégisserie, Quai de l'Ecole, Quai du Louvre, and back to the Tuileries safely, and without being known, at twenty minutes to six. The heat was intense.

We found the Emperor in the drawing-room below stairs. We changed our bonnets, and immediately re-entered the open carriages to return to St-Cloud, where we arrived about seven. The Empress could not imagine what made us so late. She looked very pretty in pink. Rested a little. A large dinner of eighty *couverts*. The Empress's three ladies, the Princesse d'Essling, Madame de Lasmarismas (a pretty English or rather Scotch lady, a Miss Macdonald), Madame de Saulecy, the Duc de Bassano (*Grand Chambellan*), the Duc de Cambacérès (*Grand Maître des Cérémonies*), the Général Rolin (*Adjutant Général du Palais*), the Comte Bacciochi (*Premier Chambellan, surintendant* of all the theatres, balls, and parties), the Comte Tascher de la Pagerie (*Premier Chambellan de l'Impératrice*), Général de Catte, Lieutenant-Colonel de Valembregne (son of Catalini[1]), Baron de Montbrun and Baron de Moraud (the four aides-de-camp of the Emperor), always dine there, and are there as well as our suite and the French gentlemen and ladies attached to us. Besides these, there were the following invitations: Prince Napoleon, Princesse Mathilde, Princesse Bacciochi (first-cousin to the Emperor by her mother, Princesse Caroline, but who belongs to the *famille civile*, and not to the *famille impérial*), the Comtesse de Montijo (the Empress's mother), the

1. Angelica Catalini, a celebrated singer.

Duchess d'Albe (the Empress's sister)...and the lady and gentleman of Princesse Mathilde and Prince Napoleon. Maréchal Vaillant also dined there.

The Empress was dressed in pink, with pearls, and I in a light full white *organdi* dress, with diamonds and blue flowers. I sat between the Emperor (whom I become more and more fond of) and Prince Napoleon (whom I can *not* get on with). At dinner the Emperor came to speak of M. Drouyn de Lhuys, and of the strange part he had acted at Vienna, of his having been at first entirely for the war and the alliance, and then afterwards not so, having even insinuated that France had not disliked to see Louis-Philippe fall, on account of his alliance with England. '*Je lui ai répondu*,' the Emperor continued, '*Louis-Philippe n'est pas tombé à cause de son alliance avec l'Angleterre, mais parce qu'il n'était pas sincère avec l'Angleterre*'. I said he was but too right in this answer, and that I could not sufficiently express our appreciation of his great *franchise*; that if there was anything to complain of, or which he felt annoyed at, he should only speak out and tell it to us, for that by these means all misunderstandings and complications would be avoided. He said he only cared '*pour les grandes choses*;' that he would not allow, at the different Courts, a French party to be kept up against the English, but that he had great difficulty in having this old and bad habit broken through; that with regard to the war, he had had great difficulties in making people in France understand that it was for the interest of France and not to please England. He was therefore peculiarly pleased and gratified at the demonstrations of enthusiasm and joy amongst all classes on our arrival, as he could not have made them show this.

After dinner the Empress presented the ladies, and we went to the theatre again, Prince Napoleon leading Vicky, and Bertie (which he was very proud of) leading Princesse Mathilde, who has taken a great fancy for him. The performance was *Un Fils de Famille*,[1] the Lancers extremely well acted; the Young Man was acted by M. Bressant, an excellent actor. After it was over, the presentations took place as last time, and we went into the gallery for a moment for refreshments.

Thursday, August 23rd

A beautiful morning. The Emperor gets telegrams constantly. The heat quite fearful the whole day, and yet one never has a headache. Breakfast as usual with the Emperor. In the breakfast-room there are three Gobelins, one of which, representing Marie-Antoinette with the Dauphin, is especially beautiful; the brilliancy of the colours is extraordinary.

Albert left directly after breakfast for Paris, to see the *Exposition*. I walked a little about the garden, close to the house, with Vicky alone, and saw the Emperor walking up one of the nearest avenues with Lord Clarendon. We walked down to the other side of the house, not far from the gate where the Zouaves were

1. A comedy by Jean-François Bayard and Charles Desnoyer de Biéville.

doing duty, and I sketched them at a distance; their dress is charming. We only remained out half an hour.

I forgot to mention that on Tuesday morning, before going to Versailles, we received the Sardinian Minister, the Marquis de Villamarina, with a General, whom the King of Sardinia had sent on purpose to compliment me, and, later, two of *les Dames de la Halle*, who brought a beautiful bouquet, and who have the right of being received. They are quite common people, but very civil. They called me '*belle Reine*,' to whom they wished all possible '*prospérités*,' as well as to my '*belle famille, sa Majesté le Prince Albert et le Prince régnant*;' and added, '*Votre demoiselle est une bien belle enfant*'.

Went when dressed, after much writing, &c. to see the dear Empress, and at half-past one started, with the Emperor and Vicky (with me in the carriage), and all our suite, for Paris. We took a turn to see the *grandes eaux* – a sort of staircase of fountains, and then the Emperor said, '*Nous irons par un autre chemin dans le Bois de Boulogne pour rester à l'ombre*'. The heat was quite tremendous, and we had to put up the head of the carriage to keep off the violence of the sun. The Emperor is always very communicative when in the carriage, and easy to get on with. He talked of the grief it had been to him to be unable to go to the Crimea, which he was sure would have been productive of such good, but that he found it impossible. There was no one whom he could leave behind who could exercise the functions of government with sufficient authority; his uncle, '*une poule mouillée*;' his cousin dangerous; in short, everything conspired to render it impossible!

We reached the Tuileries after two, where we found Albert, somewhat impatient at our non-appearance. Bertie had gone in early in private. We received Prince Napoleon and Princesse Mathilde for a moment, who came to pay their visit. They, however, left immediately, and we lunched with the Emperor and the children, quite '*à notre aise*,' upstairs. The Emperor gave Albert his rooms below, and I had the Empress's.

Directly after luncheon we all entered the Louvre, which joins the Tuileries, near the Pavillon Marsan. It is full of treasures and took us full three hours and a half going through them – unfortunately, very, very hurriedly. One ought to go there two hours every day for a week. The pictures are beautifully arranged, and you have to go through endless galleries and rooms with splendid collections of the old French, Italian, and German schools of the most celebrated masters, such as Raphael (*La belle Jardinière*), quite exquisite; magnificent Paul Veroneses, in particular, *The Supper of Cana*; Murillos, &c. &c.; and all the other great masters; a whole gallery full of pictures by Rubens; the originals of the Gobelins, representing the marriage of Marie de Médicis with Henry IV (which are at St-Cloud); very fine Flemish pictures, and modern French, &c. The weather being so very hot, and the ball of the Hôtel de Ville before us in the evening, I and two of the ladies went in little chairs, which were dragged about. (Lady Cowley

goes with us everywhere; she is staying at St-Cloud.)
We went through the Egyptian and Assyrian rooms,
where there are also great treasures; the Musée des
Desseins, with beautiful original drawings by old
masters, and very fine manuscripts; then the Musée
des Rois, which the Emperor has had chronologically
arranged, including all the relics of Napoleon, the hat
he wore at St Helena, as well as his cocked hat, his
grey great-coat and leathern breeches, &c. &c., all
which the Emperor explained to me; cloaks and boots
of Louis XVIII and Charles X; the cradle which was
used for the *Roi de Rome et le Duc de Bordeaux!* the
shoe poor Marie-Antoinette wore when she mounted
the scaffold; the ring of St Louis, which the Emperor
put on his finger, &c. &c. We looked out of three
windows, the one which commanded a beautiful view
on Paris of the Pont-Neuf and the Quais; the other
supposed to be the window out of which Charles IX
fired on the poor victims on the St Barthélemy (the
anniversary of which is to-morrow!), and one which
looks upon what is now a garden, and opposite to
which is the old and beautiful Eglise de St Germain
l'Auxerrois, under the portico of which is painted a
fine fresco. The architecture of the exterior of the
Louvre was commenced by Henri II. It is being most
beautifully carried out by the Emperor, Visconti being
the architect.

We walked down into the court, and then visited
the sculpture galleries, which are immensely rich in
beautiful antiques, and where I recognised the originals of many of our small bronzes, and of many of the

casts at Sydenham,[1] in particular the Venus of Milo. The heat was intense, and I felt a good deal over-powered. The heat rushed in as from a furnace. It was a great pity to have to see all these beautiful works of Art so hurriedly.

We got back to our rooms at seven. Rested a little. The band of the Guides was playing in the garden, and I afterwards sat writing in the Empress's little sitting-room, where there is a picture by Winter-halter of her sister on an easel. The band made me feel *wehmüthig* and melancholy. All so gay – the people cheering the Emperor as he walked up and down in the little garden – and yet how recently has blood flowed, and a whole dynasty been swept away. How uncertain is everything still! All is so beautiful here; all seems now so prosperous; the Emperor seems so fit for his place, and yet how little security one feels for the future! All depends on him and on his too precious life! These reflections crowded on my mind, and smote upon my heart, which was full of joy and gratitude for all I saw, and all the kindness we received.

The Empress's bedroom is a beautiful room, white and gold, with blue satin furniture. Next to it, the last of the suite, is her dressing-room, where I dressed – a pretty small room, but opening into the other with folding doors. There was a picture of her mother, and in a frame some beautiful long flaxen curls, which the Emperor told us were his, when a little boy. He said that they had been cut off, and that

1. *i.e.*, The Crystal Palace.

his godmother the Empress Joséphine saved them, put them into this frame, and there they are, quite safe.

Was *coiffée*, and then we had a nice, quiet *verträuliches* (cosy) little dinner with the Emperor. (The children went home to St-Cloud at seven, and were to go a little to the Empress in the evening.) We talked most cheerfully together, and he was in high spirits. We laughed so much at a fine old-fashioned Imperial *cafetière* which would not let out the coffee in spite of all the attempts of the page to make it do so. We stood – and I thought at the time how extraordinary it was, and how much had happened in those very Tuileries – with the Emperor, all three looking out of the window which opened on the garden, the sound of music, of carriages and of people being heard in the distance. We talked of past times, and the Emperor said he knew Mme Campan, who had been one of the dressers of Marie-Antoinette, and had brought up his mother. Though he could not recollect what she had herself related, he had studied her Memoirs, and in those she gave an account of how the poor Queen had been summoned to appear before the Convention and had to walk through Paris on foot; that she had lived in such dread of what would happen; also of what a hairbreadth escape she had had when the wretches entered the room, ascended the stairs, killed the *heiduc* [personal attendant], who was in bed, and were coming to her, when another called out, '*Respect aux femmes*,' to which the wretch, who was about to kill her, replied, '*Heim?*' and put up his sword. The Emperor added that Mme Campan said she could never forget this '*Heim?*' and still heard it in her ears, for with it was linked the saving of her life.

It was stiflingly hot still. We went to dress for the ball at the Hôtel de Ville, to which seven or nine thousand people had been invited. I had on my diamond diadem, with the Koh-i-noor in it, a white net dress embroidered with gold and trimmed with red geraniums, and (as were all my evening dresses) very full. It was very much admired by the Emperor and by the ladies. The Emperor asked if it was English; I said, No, it had been made on purpose in Paris.

We started with all our party, the Emperor, Albert and all the gentlemen in uniform, all the ladies very smart, for the Hôtel de Ville. The Emperor would insist on sitting backwards in the carriage, and making Albert sit next to me, which distressed my dearest Albert much; but the Emperor was so pressing and determined about it there was no resisting it. The streets were immensely full and brilliantly illuminated. In front of the Hôtel de Ville the illuminations were quite splendid, and so indeed was the whole fête; all, too, in the very best taste.

We were received and preceded by the *Préfet* and Mme Haussmann, and all the *Municipalité*. The entrance, which was decorated with flags and flowers and emblems, with fountains under the staircase, and two statues representing France and England together, was most beautiful, and, as the Emperor observed to me, '*faisait d'effet des Mille et une Nuits*'. Upstairs we found Prince Napoleon and Princesse

Mathilde, Prince Adalbert of Bavaria, and also — though they take no position before other subjects — the Countess Montijo and the Duchesse d'Albe. We went into a very fine long salon, where there was a *Haut-Pas*, with chairs. The Emperor and I sat in the middle, the Emperor to my right, then Albert to my left, with Prince Napoleon next to him, and Princesse Mathilde next the Emperor.

One quadrille of only four couples was danced: the Emperor and I with Albert and Princesse Mathilde opposite, Prince Napoleon and Madame Haussmann, and Prince Adalbert and Lady Cowley. After this there was one *valse*. Some Arabs from Algeria, fine-looking and very picturesque men, in long white bournouses, came and kissed the Emperor's hand: several kissed my hand. One in particular, a Cadi, a chieftain and priest, all in white from head to foot, with *la petite croix de la Légion d'honneur* on, was very handsome and imposing-looking.

We then made *le tour par tous les salons*, the Emperor as usual leading me, and Albert Princesse Mathilde. We went through a great many rooms, all handsomely furnished and decorated. A portion of them, however, are not new. It was quite overpoweringly hot walking through those rooms. We stopped for two or three minutes in the Salle du Trône, where Robespierre was wounded, Louis-Philippe proclaimed, and from the window of which Lamartine[1] spoke for so many hours in 1848. The Emperor said:

1. Alphonse Lamartine, poet and President of the provisional Government after the revolution of 1848.

'*Cette occasion effacera les tristes souvenirs.*' We also went down and up two other stairs to see the general effect. After taking refreshment in a small *salon* we left, Albert this time insisting on the Emperor sitting next to me. However, that was the last time, for ever afterwards, when the Empress and Vicky were not there, he always made Albert sit forwards. We went to the Tuileries. I took off my diadem which Lady Ely carried back, and we changed carriages, and were at St-Cloud by half-past twelve.

Friday, August 24th

Very little sun, but still oppressively hot, with no wind and a leaden sky. The Emperor at breakfast gave Bertie a beautiful little pistol, splendidly fitted up. Albert went off with the Emperor and Bertie to Vincennes.

Sketched a little in the room next the breakfast room, from which we very often go out, and where there is a lovely view looking up the long avenue. Afterwards writing – always so much interruption.

At half-past twelve I started with Vicky, the Princesse d'Essling and Lady Ely in the same carriage for Paris, by the road which we have often gone by. Before going we saw the dear Empress. We drove straight to the Tuileries, where we found the Emperor and Albert waiting for us, and saying it was late. We lunched immediately with him and the children, and directly afterwards went (in the town carriages) to the

Exposition, where Prince Napoleon met us, and was very gruff and contradictory as usual. We went first over to the Agricultural part, where Albert and Bertie separated from us; walked through the machinery, which is said to be very good; then inspected the various galleries, passing through the different countries, through 'Lyons', where I chose some silks, &c., through India – which is much admired . . . but only very cursorily through each. We also saw a very curious experiment on the rotation of the earth. I returned with the Emperor and Vicky to the Tuileries by a quarter to four, leaving Albert there. Rested a little. Albert returned soon after me.

At half past four we got into the carriages to proceed to the review. The Empress had arrived, but was suffering and very nervous about herself, which made the Emperor very anxious. She looked very pale, dressed all in pink, but she soon forgot all about her health, said she felt well, and was in high spirits. She and the two children, Bertie in his full Highland dress, were in the carriage with us. The Emperor, Albert, Prince Adalbert, Prince Napoleon, and a most brilliant suite, were all on horseback. The Emperor rode by my side, and Albert by the Empress's. There were immense and most enthusiastic crowds. We proceeded by that beautiful Place de la Concorde to the Champ-de-Mars over the Pont d'Jéna. A few drops of rain fell, but nothing to signify. The *coup-d'œil* in the Champ-de-Mars was truly magnificent: from thirty to forty thousand men – several rows deep – each regiment with its powerful, good band, and their fine commanding *tambours-majors*, fine bearded *sapeurs* (those of the *Voltigeurs de la Garde* have yellow *tabliers*), and the very picturesque and smartly dressed *cantinières*, some of whom were particularly smart, all cheering and all playing *God Save the Queen*.

The cortège had become immense as we drove down the lines (only in the middle, as it would have taken too much time otherwise), having been increased by the marshals, generals (Canrobert included), and the picturesque Arabs. We first passed down the infantry, then the cavalry, which is beautiful, and then the artillery. This over, we drove into the Ecole Militaire, the Emperor alone getting off and handing me upstairs to the large balcony, in front of which the Emperor, Albert, &c. took their station. There we found Princesse Mathilde, and sat down. Then they began to *défiler* in quick time, which took three-quarters of an hour; and beautiful it was – such fine troops.

The infantry came first, commencing with the Zouaves and *Chasseurs de la Garde*, very pretty indeed (the *cantinières* belonging to them wear the full trouser without the petticoat, like the men), then the Cavalry Guides (a very fine regiment), the *Cuirassiers de la Garde*, *Carabiniers*, *Cent-Gardes* (of which there are a hundred only, all non-commissioned officers, who always do the duty in the Palace), the *Carabiniers*, two regiments, one of which we saw at Eu, *Lanciers*, *Hussards*, *Gendarmerie*, very fine, and lastly artillery – which is just the reverse with us, where the Artillery come first. The clothes of all the men are infinitely

better made and cut than those of ours, which pro-
vokes me much. The drums (brass ones) are also
much finer than ours. It was a beautiful sight. Albert
regretted, and so did I, that I was not on horseback.

This over (it kept dropping rain all the time), I
took leave of the dear Empress, and the Emperor
came to fetch me, and I told him how delighted I had
been to see these splendid troops, *qui étaient les
camarades de ces braves troupes qui se battaient à côté des
miennes,*' and that I had a real affection for them. The
Emperor replied, he hoped that this happy unity
would ever continue, and that I should be able to look
at them as if they were my own. Princesse Mathilde
got into the carriage with the children and me, and we
drove away. The scene, looking back on that magnificent Champ-de-Mars, glittering with those thousands
of troops, and the brilliant cortège, was dazzling and
brilliant in the extreme. It was still very hot.

We drove straight to the Hôtel des Invalides, under
the dome of which Napoléon lies, late as it was, as
we were most anxious not to miss this, perhaps the
most important act of all in this very interesting and
eventful time. It was nearly seven when we arrived
there. All the old Invalides, chiefly of the former,
though some of the present, war, were drawn up on
either side of the court into which we drove. It seems
we had not been expected, there having been some
mistake on account of the change of hour for the
Review, which was to have been in the morning, but
which, in consequence of the fearful heat, the Emperor
had put off to five o'clock, and that wicked Prince

Napoleon had hoped (for he hinted to Albert that there would be no time) that we should not go – I fully believe, in the hope that it would hurt the Emperor. The Governor, Comte d'Ornano, was in a great state at not having been *prévenu*. However, it all did very well.

There were four torches which lit us along, and added to the solemnity of the scene, which was striking in every way. The church is fine and lofty. We went to look from above into the open vault, the effect of which the Emperor does not like, as he says it looks like *'un grand bassin,'* and *'on arrive et on se demande qui est dans le tombeau de l'Empereur, on s'attend à voir de l'eau ici'*. The work and interior designs are, however, very fine. The coffin is not yet there, but in a small side chapel, de St Jérôme, not below. Into this the Emperor led me, and there I stood, at the arm of Napoleon III his nephew, before the coffin of our bitterest foe, I, the granddaughter of that King who hated him most and who most vigorously opposed him, and this very nephew, who bears his name, being my nearest and dearest ally!

The organ of the Invalides was playing *God Save the Queen* at the time, and this solemn scene took place by torchlight (accidentally). Strange and wonderful indeed! It seems as if, in this tribute of respect to a departed and great foe, old enmities and rivalries were wiped out, and the seal of heaven placed upon that bond of amity which is now happily established between two great and powerful nations! May Heaven bless and prosper it!

The coffin is covered with black velvet and gold, and the Emperor's orders, hat, and sword are placed at its foot. The Emperor does not intend to bury him here, but to take him to St-Denis, where all the French kings are buried, his great wish being to legalise the family as a dynasty in France.[1] He will leave the heart here. We went down into the vault for a moment, but it was very cold. We then left and returned to the Tuileries by half-past seven, when Princesse Mathilde and the Princes took leave of us.

We had our nice *verträuliches* little dinner with the Emperor (the children had again gone home), and we began talking a great deal about the war. Some despatches had arrived up to the 14th, and Albert showed the Emperor the 'morning state,' and spoke of the reports we had received. The servants being still in the room, the Emperor began to talk in English. He lamented bitterly the want of invention and energy in both our commanders from the first, and the absence of any great genius. He then spoke very openly and very frankly of the defects of our generals, and we told him equally frankly of what was objected to his; and nothing could be more satisfactory than the conversation, or more straightforward or

1. The eldest brother of Napoleon III, who was a great favourite of Napoleon I, was buried by his uncle's orders at St-Denis, where a monument was erected to his memory. When the Emperor fell, Louis XVIII had both the remains and the tomb removed. Napoleon III, by a decree of November, 1858, ordained that the Imperial dynasty should have its vault at St-Denis. This vault was actually constructed, but no attempt was made to remove the remains of Napoleon I from the Invalides.

honest than the Emperor's observations and propositions. It was just as if we had one and the same army,
and so in fact it is; but it is very pleasant to find this
feeling in another sovereign.

It was pretty to hear the *retraite*, which sent the
people (long after dark) out of the gardens of the
Tuileries.

At half-past nine we went with the Emperor, &c.,
to the Opéra-Comique, not in state, though we were
recognised. We were in the Emperor's private box,
which is on the stage. Only Lady Ely, Mme Labédoyère (a charming person), Lord Clarendon, Maréchal Vaillant, and Count Bacciochi were in the box
with us. It was Auber's pretty opera of *Haydée*, very
nicely sung. The first act was over when we arrived.
After the opera, before the curtain dropped, *God Save
the Queen* was sung, and I was obliged to show myself,
and was loudly cheered.

We drove back to St-Cloud by half-past twelve.
The Emperor talked much of the war in the carriage.
He had received despatches. It had rained heavily.

Saturday, August 25th

The air cooled and refreshed by the rain in the
night; dull early. The Emperor was much pleased by
two stereoscopic views of the visit to Sydenham, when
he and the Empress were there,[1] which I gave him.
Busy writing. Went for a moment, when dressed to

1. See pp. 56–8.

go to St-Germain, to see the dear Empress, who was in bed with nothing on her head, and her hair merely twisted and combed back, but looking very pretty, with her very funny, very little dog, a little Cuba one, and a dear little thing called Linda, which the Empress generally carries on her arm, on her bed. The Emperor was there. She was well.

We started at half-past eleven for the Forêt de St-Germain with the whole party but Lord Clarendon, who could not go – we, with the Emperor and Vicky in our carriage. We drove from the garden door *en poste* through the park of St-Cloud, along a charming road through a beautiful country by a small village called La Celle St-Cloud, with pretty country houses near it, decorated, as every village was which we went through, and by Bougival, full of people who presented bouquets, including generally *les autorités*, *le curé*, &c., with arches and banners and all sorts of kind mottoes. The NEVA which they wrote here without any stops, makes *Neva*, which struck the Emperor so much in London, and had done so already at Boulogne last year. As you pass through this village the view becomes beautiful, very extensive, richly wooded, the houses with flat roofs towering one above the other. It struck Albert as very Italian-looking.

We next came to Marly, or at least to La Machine de Marly on the Seine, along which the road goes. It is very pretty, and there are many country houses here. At Marly another arch, and bouquets and an address presented. Soon after this we entered La Forêt de Saint-Germain, innumerable avenues, which at certain parts of the forest meet in a sort of cross, from which a great number of roads branch off up other avenues. This is very like the Forêt d'Eu, near Eu, which the poor King[1] took us to, and was so fond and proud of, having lately bought it! It was dreadfully dusty, the soil being very sandy (this is the case everywhere here, and makes it very healthy). The sun had come out, and altogether it became oppressive.

We arrived at about half-past one, or a little before, at La Muette, a small *rendezvous de chasse* with a few rooms in it, which were again all ready and prepared for us. Maréchal Magnan (*Grand Veneur*[2]), Comte Edgar Ney[3], M. de Toulongeon, &c., all in the huntsmen's dress, dark green velvet with red waistcoats, high boots and cocked hats, received us there. Many people from the neighbourhood were assembled, including good old Lablache, who was called up for us to speak to, and who wept when the Emperor shook hands with him, and said: '*La Reine m'a recommandé votre fils.*'

The dogs with the huntsmen were then brought up, and they played a fanfare on horns. Some *jeunes filles*, dressed all in white with green wreaths, then asked permission to present me with a nosegay and some fruit, and they came accompanied by the *curé*, &c. One of them, a very young girl, began a long

1. In 1843 and again in 1845, the Queen and Prince Albert visited King Louis-Philippe at the Château d'Eu.
2. Master of the Royal Hunt.
3. Aide-de-camp to Napoleon III.

speech, bringing in our visit, the alliance, the *Exposition*, &c., and stopped suddenly, saying: '*Ah, mon Dieu!*' The Emperor and I proposed to relieve her by taking the nosegay from her and thanking her; but she would *not* give it up, and said: '*Attendez, je vais me rappeler,*' which nearly set us off; but she persevered, and did recollect it. She broke down, however, a second time; and then the *curé*, who had evidently composed the speech, burst forth with the finale of '*Vive la Reine d'Angleterre!*' which set the girl right again, and she continued: '*Vive la Reine d'Angleterre, vive sa Demoiselle, vive son Prince Albert, vive l'Empereur, vive l'Impératrice, vive tout le monde!*' We laughed much afterwards, for the effect was so funny, and yet the poor girl was much to be pitied, and admired for her courage and perseverance. She looked so frightened.

After this we took luncheon, with only the Emperor and the two children, in a small room, next to where the others were lunching. The band of the *Gardes* played on the terrace in front of the house, and the huntsmen played fanfares. They are also dressed in dark green and gold, with red waistcoats and white gaiters. The *Gardes-chasse* were in dark green, with brown gaiters and cocked hats. The *gendarmes* too looked very handsome.

The Emperor gave us yesterday some excellent German beer, which he has had brewed on purpose, and which delighted Albert. The fowl and *bouillon* are quite delicious, and the *cuisine* generally is simple and good, but with less variety than ours.

After luncheon, and talking together some little time, we went into the front room or hall, where we sat down, and I sketched a little and listened to the music, which was very pretty. The Emperor was very gay, and danced with the children. We left again about half-past three, drove along through the fine forest, and along the terrace of St-Germain, which commands a most beautiful and extensive view, and where we stopped for one moment to look at a sketch a man was making. We drove straight up to the old Palace of St-Germain. Its position is fine. Here Louis XIV used originally to live, and the early kings also had their residence. Mdlle de la Vallière lived here, and also our James II, who died here, and is buried in the church, which, however, we did not go to see. The palace has latterly been used as a barrack and a prison. We got out and went up to see it, particularly the rooms of James II and La Vallière. The Emperor has lately recovered the property, and intends to try and do something with it; but he was much disgusted when he saw the state of ruin and filth in which it is.

From here we returned direct to St-Cloud, by quite another road, through Chaton, beautifully decorated, where a nosegay was presented to us. Leaving Nanterre at a little distance, Rueil not far, from which numberless nosegays and baskets by *jeunes filles*, &c., were handed to us, and which is not far from Malmaison of which we caught a glimpse, and where everything reminds you, as the Emperor said, of the Empress Joséphine. He remembers quite well going to see her there, and staying there. Queen Christina[1] generally lives there now, but had left before our arrival. We came through a number of vineyards, which are very picturesque, and also to le Mont Valérien, which was fortified by Louis-Philippe at the time he built the fortifications of Paris. The view of Paris was magnificent again this evening, but the sky looked very heavy and threatening. We got home at a quarter to six. The dear Empress was in the garden when we returned. She was then going to dine, and go to Versailles, to dress there for the ball.

Rested, but had to choose quantities of Lyons silks &c., while I was lying on the nice sofa. Was *coiffée* with diamonds (no diadem) and flowers before dinner.

We dined with the Emperor and Vicky. Albert had not been quite well, and therefore starved himself. Our dinner was before eight. After it we dressed. I had a white *organdi* embroidered dress trimmed with bouquets of flowers, and Vicky (who all along looked nice in her different smart dresses) in a net dress over white, trimmed with blush roses.

At a quarter-past nine we all started, we, with the Emperor and Vicky, the *piqueurs* carrying torches, which I had not seen since I was in Germany. It twice rained while we were on the way, which alarmed us, but entirely cleared before we reached Versailles, the moon shining beautifully. The palace looked magnificent, entirely illuminated with lamps,

1. Mother of Isabella II of Spain, then living in exile in France.

which had a charming effect. The staircase, finely lighted up and carpeted, looked quite different from what [*sic*] we had previously seen it. The dear Empress met us at the top of the staircase, looking really like a fairy queen or nymph, in a white dress trimmed with branches of *grass* and diamonds; a beautiful *tour de corsage* of diamonds round the top of her dress, and all *en rivière*; the same round her waist, and a corresponding coiffure, with her Spanish and Portuguese Orders. The Emperor said when she appeared, '*Comme tu es belle!*'

We stopped a moment to take off our *mantilles*, and then, having seen that all our attendants were there, we went through the Galerie des Glaces, which was full of people and one blaze of light from innumerable lustres, wreaths of flowers being hung from the ceiling. We went to the window to look at the illuminations, all along the *grillage*, of yellow and green lamps, with our four initials at intervals, which were reflected in the water in the most beautiful manner. The effect was quite splendid. We next went into another room, from the balcony of which we witnessed the fireworks, which were magnificent; rockets and bouquets of girandoles, the like of which I have never before seen – they went so high, and the balls and lights thrown were so variegated in colours. Guns were fired the whole time, and unfortunately the smoke was driven by the wind too low, which slightly obscured the fireworks at the end, to the great distress of the poor Empress, who had planned and designed these, as well as the whole fête. The Emperor had,

I believe, ordered the guns, as he thought (and in that he was right) that one always required something to keep up the excitement. The finale was the representation in fireworks of Windsor Castle, a very pretty attention. We then returned to the ball, and the dancing began.

The Empress did not dance. I danced the first quadrille with the Emperor, Albert being my *vis-à-vis* with Princesse Mathilde; Vicky dancing with Prince Napoleon, and Bertie with the Duchesse d'Albe, Prince Adalbert with the Princess of Augustenburg (daughter of the Prince of Noer, who was there), and Comte Walewski with Lady Cowley. A valse followed this, the Emperor valsing with Vicky, and Albert with the Princess of Augustenburg. Then another quadrille, which I danced with Prince Napoleon, the Emperor being our *vis-à-vis* with Comtesse Walewska, Albert dancing with the Duchess of Alba, Vicky with Prince Adalbert, and Bertie with Princesse Mathilde. Several people – foreigners, Germans – were brought up to me, and presented, having first been presented to the Emperor and Empress; amongst others Victor, Duke of Ratibor, eldest brother to Thesy and Amalie Schillingsfürst,[1] an old friend of Albert's and an acquaintance of mine. Count Bismarck, Prussian Minister at Frankfort, and very Russian and *Kreuzzeitung*,[2] was presented, and on my observing how

1. Princesses Thérèse and Amalie Hohenlohe-Schillingsfürst.
2. A reference to the Prussian Junker party, who named themselves after the newspaper *Kreuzzeitung* which supported their policy.

beautiful Paris was, he said, '*Sogar schöner wie Petersburg*'.

I valsed next with the Emperor, who valses very quietly, and the two children together, and then danced a quadrille with Victor Ratibor, the Emperor dancing *vis-à-vis* with [blank in original] and Albert with Mme Labédoyère. The children also danced. The Arabs were all there, Fanny Gainsborough[1] also, to my great astonishment, but very few English.

This over, we waited in the celebrated Œil-de-bœuf, where Louis XIV's courtiers waited for him, *pour être au lever*, and which the ball-room opens into. It was beautifully *meublé* for the occasion, with Beauvais furniture, &c. We waited till all the company had gone in to supper, and then began our procession, the Guard's officers, &c. walking before us.

(Buckingham Palace, September 5th – I am writing this here, where we came to-day on our way to Scotland.) We walked through a number of fine rooms and a long gallery to the theatre, where the supper was. The sight was truly magnificent. The whole stage was covered in, and four hundred people sat down to supper at forty small tables of ten each, each presided over by a lady and nicely selected – all by the Empress's own desire and arrangement. The whole was beautifully lit up with countless chandeliers, and decorated with many garlands of flowers. The boxes were full of spectators, and a band was playing, but not visible. We sat at a small table in the

1. Frances, Countess of Gainsborough, Lady of the Bedchamber.

[126]

centre box, only with the Emperor and Empress, the two children, Prince Napoleon, Princesse Mathilde, and Prince Adalbert.

It was quite one of the finest and most magnificent sights we have ever witnessed. There had not been a ball at Versailles since the time of Louis XVI, and the design of this one had been taken from a print of a fête given by Louis XV.

The supper over, we returned to the Salle des Glaces, where there was one more valse, which the Emperor danced with Vicky.

The Emperor presented the Prince of Noer to me. He is brother to the Duke of Augustenburg, and is like him, and like the pictures of George II's family – not pleasing.

It was near two when we left. I put on my cloak in a very pretty little room, which had been *meublée* for the occasion, and in which Marie-Antoinette used to live. The Empress looked lovely. She came home in the carriage with the Emperor and ourselves, and was very merry. She is so amiable. The Emperor, as he led me away, said: '*C'est terrible que ce soit l'avant-dernier soir.*' For this I was equally sorry. I observed, I hoped he would come to England again, to which he replied, 'Most certainly!' and: '*Mais n'est-ce pas, vous reviendrez? Comme nous nous connaissons maintenant, nous pouvons aller nous voir à Windsor et à Fontaine-bleau sans grande cérémonie, n'est-ce pas?*' I replied that this would give me great pleasure, which it certainly would. He is particularly anxious we should come to Fontainebleau, which we could not go to this time.

It was half-past two when we got home, much delighted – the children in ecstasies – and past three before we got to bed.

Sunday, August 26th

This *dearest* of days [Prince Albert's birthday] was not ushered in as usual, nor spent as I could have wished, but my dear Albert was pleased, and it was spent with those who do appreciate him as they ought. May God ever bless and protect him for many, many years to come, and may we ever be together to our lives' end! The morning was beautiful, and when I was dressed, dear Albert came in. I gave him, on a table surrounded by a wreath, a very fine bronze of the celebrated Belgian group, *Le Lion Amoureux*, and some pretty little Alliance and Crimean studs, the third button having a blank, I hope for Sevastopol. The Emperor joined us, and we breakfasted.

Immediately after breakfast, the Emperor said that he had some music of his own composition in honour of Albert's birthday, and he took us on to the balcony in Albert's dressing-room, which overlooks the court, where were assembled three hundred drummers, with their several *tambours-majors*. When we appeared, the Emperor gave them the signal: '*Commencez!*' and they all, as if but one man, began a splendid roll of drums in a particular manner, which they only do '*le jour de l'an*'. They repeated this twice, and then went away cheering. It was very fine, and very kind of the

[128]

Emperor to think of it. He is himself particularly fond of it.

After this I asked the Emperor if we might drive again a little. The phaetons were ordered up directly, and I got into the first with the Emperor, who drove me, Albert going in the second with the children. He was unfortunately still not very well. The Emperor drove us about in the charming cool avenues of the park of this most enjoyable, delightful palace of St-Cloud. There are a good many roedeer running wild about, and also fallow-deer; and the Emperor says there is good pheasant-shooting. While we were driving, I talked to the Emperor of Prince Napoleon and my fear that he was *bien méchant,* which the Emperor would not admit, but said that he certainly had the unhappy talent of saying everything that was most disagreeable, and offended everyone. A little while after I said to him that, as the Emperor was always so very frank in all he said to me, and wished that I should be the same, I was very anxious to tell him something, *'que j'avais bien à cœur qu'il comprît,'* and this was that he should understand on what footing I was with the Orléans family; – that they were my friends and relations, and that I could not drop them in their adversity, but that they were very discreet, and that politics were not touched upon between us. The Emperor replied that he quite understood this, and felt that I could not abandon those who were in misfortune. I added that I felt certain that this was the Emperor's feeling, but that other people tried, and Walewski was one, to make a great deal of it,

[129]

1

and to make me understand that the Emperor would
be very much displeased. He said that that was just
like Walewski (who he laments should not be more
'capable'). *'Comme nous sommes une fois sur ce sujet,'* he
continued, he wished to explain the motives which
led him to confiscate the property of the Orléans
family, a step which had been much attacked. That he
had *'aucune animosité'* towards the *famille d'Orléans*,
that he had wished to leave all the Orléanist *employés*
in their places, to displace no one, and to receive
every one, but that he had discovered that their
agents, encouraged by themselves (though on my
observation that I was sure they would not conspire,
he admitted that), were attempting to upset his
authority, and that then he felt that he could not
leave them with such large possessions, which would
give them the power to use them against the Government. He had therefore pursued the same course
which had been pursued before of obliging them to
sell their property within six months, but he repeated
that he had *'aucune animosité,'* and he hoped I had told
the Queen [Marie-Amélie] that it would give him
pleasure if she passed through France on her way to
Spain. I could not make much further remark beyond
saying that they had felt the confiscation very much,
and that they were much more bitter in consequence
– at least they had been at the time, for now the subject never was mentioned between us. I praised the
Princes and the Queen, their discretion, &c. The
Emperor said, in conclusion of his explanation about
the confiscation, that their agents were in constant

communication with his enemies, even *'avec ceux qui prêchent l'assassinât.'* I said I could hardly credit this; they were incapable of any such act, I was sure. I however added, that naturally all exiles were inclined to conspire, which he did not deny, and which he had practised, in fact, himself.

We talked of the poor Duke of Orléans and his death.[1] I said that my poor dear Aunt Louise (Queen of the Belgians) had said, when this took place, that she knew that the fate of her family was sealed. The Emperor continued: *'Je voudrais bien savoir ce qu'était véritablement Louis-Philippe? Si c'était un brave homme. Bien des personnes disent que c'était ce qu'on appelle un bonhomme tout-à-fait, et d'autres disent que ce n'était que de la finesse.'* I replied, that perhaps he was neither the one nor the other; that he was very kind, and had most amiable qualities, but that I thought he had not the appreciation of right and wrong in political matters which we should consider necessary, as, for instance, in the Spanish marriages.[2]

A curious conversation, but which I was greatly relieved to have had; for, with my feelings of sincerity, I could not bear that there should be anything between us, now that the alliance is so firmly and intimately established, and still more since we personally are on so intimate and friendly a footing. I was

1. In June 1842, Ferdinand, Duke of Orléans, was thrown from his phaeton at Neuilly and died shortly afterwards.
2. A reference to attempts fostered by King Louis-Philippe to revive the traditional Bourbon policy of French predominance in Spain.

very anxious to get this out, and not to have that untouchable ground between us; indeed Stockmar, as far back as last winter, suggested and advised that this course should be pursued. The Emperor during the conversation proposed (which he had already done last Sunday) to take us to see the Chapelle de St-Ferdinand, built on the spot where the poor Duke of Orléans died.

We drove to Villeneuve-l'Etang, where we got out, visited the dairy (excessively pretty) and Swiss farm which is also very pretty (both quite new), with a cow-stable built on the same plan as our cow-stables.

The house is small but charming; only furnished with chintz, but with all sorts of pretty pictures and prints upstairs. This reminded me of Osborne and of the old house – I do not mean the house itself, but the way in which the Emperor had collected all sorts of pictures and put them into this house. He showed us also some sorts of boats, or enormous shoes, into which you put your feet, and by means of balancing an oar get quite easily and safely along the water. We only got home at half-past eleven.

At twelve, service was read, as last Sunday, only without a sermon. We lunched at half-past one with the Emperor and Empress. Both most kindly gave Albert presents; the former a beautiful picture by Meissonier, the finest thing in the Exhibition, and with which Albert was in ecstasies. It cost 25,000 frs. – 1,000 l. The Emperor kept constantly asking me, through Lady Ely, what Albert would like to have, and I said at last, I knew how Albert admired this picture, and the Emperor instantly sent for it and gave it to him. So very kind! The Empress gave him a beautiful *pocale*, carved in ivory and handsomely mounted. The presents were placed in the luncheon room. Last Sunday the Empress gave me a beautiful bouquet-holder of diamonds, pearls, and rubies, with the stems of enamel. She said nothing beyond hoping I would take the bouquet; and I felt shy about accepting it, and inquired through my dresser of her dresser, who then said she hoped I would retain it. It is quite lovely.

After our luncheon we received old Prince Jérôme, father to Prince Napoleon, and the only remaining brother of the late Emperor. He is an odd old man, and I believe would not come and be there during our visit, on account of his *position de Roi*.[1] He is now seventy-two. The son is like him. He is rather tall, and very civil, but not *distingué*-looking. Albert knew him well at Florence in the winter of 1838. He was in uniform.

Busy writing, &c. Saw for a moment the Duchesse de Bassano, and then Mme de Montebello, who has lost a near and dear relative, and could therefore not have *le service* about me, which she was to have had.

At a quarter-past four we drove out in five phaetons, two of them two-seated, in the first of which the Emperor (driving himself) went with Albert; in the second the dear Empress went with me. We drove to the Bois de Boulogne. You must always go through the town or village of Boulogne,

1. From 1807–13 he was King of Westphalia.

which joins on to the bridge of St-Cloud, and there were generally many soldiers there, Zouaves, *Gardes*, &c. There are here large gigantic omnibuses, which are put upon rails and which, by the help of two horses, go backwards and forwards to Paris. Seventy people can go in one of them. The Bois de Boulogne was full of people and equipages, and so gay; the evening so fine, alas! alas! our last. The view from the bridge of St-Cloud, looking up and down the river, of Paris, and of the palace and park of St-Cloud, is truly beautiful. There is a steamer which carries people from Paris to St-Cloud. The Emperor has also a small private steamer, which was illuminated the night we arrived.

We drove through the Bois de Boulogne, along the Route de la Révolte, which was where the horses ran away with the poor Duke of Orléans' carriage. We came to the small chapel which is on the Boulevard de Neuilly, and here we got out. It is enclosed within a railing, and is a low but very beautiful little chapel, in the ancient Lombard Gothic style, resembling a mausoleum. The interior is very striking, small as it is. As you enter, you face the high altar, over which is a fine 'Descent of the Cross' in marble, by Triqueti, and behind it painted windows. On the left is another altar, dedicated to St-Ferdinand, and on the right, corresponding to that, is the beautiful and touching monument, by Triqueti, of the poor Duke of Orléans. He is represented just as he was on his deathbed, in his uniform, and with the expression of death on his countenance. At the head is a kneeling angel with upstretched hands, as if imploring heaven for mercy. This was the work of poor Marie.[1] There are bas-reliefs round the basement. It is most touching. Behind the altar there are a few steps to lead to the very small sacristy, in which there is a picture by Guagnard, representing the sad tragedy of the Duke's death as it really happened, with portraits of all those present. It is most sad. The whole interior of the chapel is in black and white marble, and the *prie-Dieu*, &c., are all in black; two, worked in black and silver, are the work of the poor Queen and Louise.[2] Where the chapel now stands was the house of an *épicier*, into which poor Chartres [*sic*] was carried. The King purchased it and the surrounding ground, and had this chapel erected within about a year afterwards.

The Emperor led me about, and was very kind and feeling. As we came out a woman from the opposite house, where the *curé* who attended us lives, brought two medals in a box, which the Emperor took from her, paying for them himself and giving them to me *comme souvenir*. They contained the heads of poor Chartres and [the Comte de] Paris, with some lines in allusion to the latter being the hope of France! and on the back of the other there is a representation of the chapel. Strange for the Emperor to have bought them!

We got into the carriage again, and then drove

1. Duchess Alexander of Würtemberg, second daughter of King Louis-Philippe.
2. First daughter of King Louis-Philippe, late Queen of the Belgians and second wife of Leopold I.

about in the Bois de Boulogne, and afterwards, at
my request, in the park of St-Cloud (the *parc
réservé*) round the terrace overlooking Paris, where the
view on this, alas! *last* evening was more beautiful
than ever. While driving I had a great deal of conversation with the dear Empress, who is good, clever,
and sensible, as well as lovely and attractive. The
first part of the conversation was about Prince
Napoleon and Princesse Mathilde, and their being
such a difficulty and such a disadvantage to them.
That he was disliked by everyone, by none more than
by those very *ouvriers* whose names he was always
invoking. That the father was entirely in the hands
of the son, always wanting the Emperor to make him
more beloved! That he wanted mention to have been
made of him at Inkermann, though he had not been
engaged, having been ill! and both father and son
were very angry with poor Canrobert about it. He
would not go back to the Crimea, as he ought to have
done, but chose to remain at Paris. The other part of
the conversation was after we had been to the
Chapelle de St-Ferdinand, and was about the poor
Orléans family, I telling her that I had been speaking
to the Emperor on the subject in the morning, and
that he had been explaining to me the cause of the
confiscation; that I regretted it, and that it had embittered the family greatly; that I thought a seques-
tration would have placed them more in his power,
and would have been less harsh. She said after a
pause: '*J'ai bien regretté cette affaire des biens.*' She
then praised the Queen very much, said she was very

much beloved in France still, but that the way in which the family had left France had done them great harm. She had heard all the details from M. Delessert, one of the King's ministers (who does not come to Court), who had described the Queen as very courageous; that if the King had only not left the country, and had made a stand at Mont Valérien,[1] all would have been prevented! Aumale[2] and Joinville. whom she knew at Seville, she praised very much, When the Queen Amélie was in Spain last year, her [Empress Eugénie's] mother, the Comtesse de Montijo, and the Duchesse d'Albe, were there, and they did not know what to do. The Queen having been very kind to the Duchesse d'Albe, who was married in Paris, and having, I understood, known the Duc d'Albe or his mother, they did not wish to be wanting in respect towards her. They therefore in perplexity inquired whether they should pay their respects, and the Queen said they should, and they were very kindly received by her.

I repeated to the Empress what I told to the Emperor about my reception of the Orléans family and the footing on which I was with them, and which

1. On February 24, 1848, Louis-Philippe's second son, the Duc de Nemours, offered to conduct the Duchesse d'Orléans, Louis-Philippe's daughter-in-law, and her children to the fort at Mont Valérien under the protection of an artillery regiment, but this offer was refused. On Louis-Philippe's abdication, the Duchesse had been declared regent and her son, the Comte de Paris, heir to the throne. Realising that he had been abandoned by the Garde Nationale, Louis-Philippe decided that he would put up no defence.

2. Général Duc d'Aumale, fourth son of King Louis-Philippe.

[137]

I was anxious he should understand. When I said this, she replied, this was quite natural; the Emperor never could object to it, and that *'ce serait très-mal même, si vous ne les voyiez pas'*. Nothing could be nicer, kinder, or more *right-minded* and noble than all she said; and I am sure that she will ever give him good and mild advice.

I cannot say how much these two conversations have relieved me; for, knowing the Emperor and Empress as well as I do, and having become really so very fond of them both, I should be distressed *s'il y avait quelque chose entre nous*, in which he could regard us with distrust.

The Empress and I also talked of those Spanish marriages, and the misfortune they had brought upon Spain, and on Louis-Philippe himself.

It was still beautiful when we came home, and I stood for a moment with the Emperor on our balcony, looking on the *Cent-Gardes*, who were feeding the swans and the very old carps in the *bassins* just under the windows. Rested, and wrote in my room, not believing it could be the last evening.

We dined earlier – about half-past seven. No additions to the dinner. Before it, Albert gave snuff-boxes to the gentlemen who had been with us, to Maréchal Vaillant and Général Rollin; and I gave handsome bracelets to the ladies about me, and the good and amiable Princesse d'Essling.

The dear Empress had a white net dress with cerise or pink trimmings and a wreath of pink *pensées* in her hair, and I a white net dress, with bunches of pink acacia, and my Indian diadem, ornaments and pearls, which the Emperor and Empress much admired. I sat between the Emperor and Maréchal Vaillant. The good old Marshal, to whom I expressed, as I did to everyone I spoke to, my delight at the reception I had met with, my sorrow at going and my hope to return, said that for him, who had lived long enough to remember many different dynasties and feelings in the country, to see the hearty and sincere *rapprochement* of the two nations was one of the most extraordinary things which could be imagined, and that the effect of it would be *very great*. I spoke of Prince Napoleon and his *not* being amiable, and he did not attempt to conceal his aversion for him, but said there was not the slightest chance of his ever succeeding the Emperor. We must pray and hope that the Emperor's life may be spared long enough to enable his son, should he have one, to be grown up and able to succeed. The Marshal was, and so I believe were others, *not* pleased at my having given Prince Napoleon the Bath: '*C'était bien bon à Votre Majesté de lui donner l'ordre du Bain; ce n'est pas à moi de critiquer les actes de Votre Majesté, mais —*' He evidently thought it was throwing it away.

Prince Napoleon and Princesse Mathilde came after dinner, and so did Prince Adalbert, rather later, and when the concert had already begun, just in time and very *à propos* to hear *Les Ruines d'Athènes* by Beethoven. '*Son cheval s'était trouvé mal,*' he said, and had been unable to proceed with him, so that he had been obliged to go back and get another. The concert took place in the *Orangerie*. It was a fine one, inter-mingled with choruses by members of the Conservatoire of good music by Beethoven, Mendelssohn, Marcello, &c., which Albert was much pleased with, but which bored the Emperor. Old Auber, whom we had not seen since we were at Eu in 1843, was there.

In this very *Orangerie* the celebrated *Révolution du 18 Brumaire* (Nov. 10th), 1799, took place, and all the Convention jumped out of the windows. Prince Napoleon was christened at St-Cloud, and Napoleon I's *mariage civil* took place here. Charles X signed his abdication here, and here Jacques Clément assassinated Henri III. The château, as it now stands, was purchased by Louis XIV for his brother Monsieur. Everywhere one walks on classical, alas! too often bloody ground. Oh! if our visit might be the beginning of more internal peace and tranquillity!

St-Cloud, Monday, August 27th

Though my account of this delightful and never-to-be-forgotten week, the record of which will go down, everyone says, to history as *le drap d'or*, will not be completed for some days, I must write to-day, and here in my lovely dressing-room, in this beautiful St-Cloud, with the cool sound of the fountains in my ear, a few parting words! I am deeply grateful for these very happy eight days, and for the delight of seeing such beautiful and interesting places and objects, and for the reception we have met with at

Paris, and in France generally. Such a reception is most significant. The union of the two nations and of the two sovereigns, for there is a great friendship sprung up between us, is of the greatest importance. May God bless these two countries, and may He specially protect the precious life of the Emperor! May this happy union ever continue for the benefit of the world!

A beautiful morning, which made the dear place only look more lovely, and the departure even more sad. I got up earlier, and for the last time heard the joyous sound of the muster of the Guard. Everything in my lovely room was beautifully arranged and furnished. The toilette of the finest *point d'Angleterre*, with choice ornaments, beautiful modern Sèvres china, with my initials on the washing-stand, gold and glass tumblers and bottles, which they insisted on my taking with me. In the sitting-room, charming light green satin furniture, and a beautiful *écritoire* (which I wrote at). Several pictures hung in the rooms are taken from the Louvre on purpose. In the *salon* (which was a charming room) there were four windows, besides one over the fire-place, which shut up as a looking-glass. The room projects, which caused the window on each side. There was some beautiful furniture of Beauvais manufacture on a red ground in it. *Parquets* in all the rooms.

The Emperor took us down, after our last nice breakfast, to look at a beautiful statue by Poullet, which is at the bottom of the smaller staircase. It represents Night, a rising female figure only supported by the drapery. In the other, or principal hall, there is a very fine statue by Pradier, a sitting female figure. I gave the Emperor some photographs of Albert and Vicky, which pleased him. He afterwards went out for a moment into the garden with us, and gave me an orange flower and leaf to dry for my collection. At length, at ten, we were ready to go, and the Emperor came, saying the Empress was ready, but *'ne peut s'arracher,'* and that, if I would come to her room, it would make her come. When we came in, the Emperor called to her, *'Eugénie, la Reine est là;'* and she came and gave me a beautiful fan, and a rose and heliotrope from the garden, and Vicky a beautiful bracelet set with rubies and diamonds, containing her hair, with which Vicky was delighted.

We started at half-past ten, the Emperor and Empress going in the carriage with us. I was so grieved to leave that charming St-Cloud. The morning was more beautiful than ever, though tremendously hot. The crowds were great everywhere and most friendly, beginning in the town of St-Cloud, where we generally (as also in other places) saw some poor wounded soldiers from the Crimea, including some of my favourites, the Zouaves. The Arc de Triomphe, under which we drove almost daily, had never been driven under by anyone before, except, I think, by the Emperor himself on one great occasion, and when the celebrated *'cendres de Napoléon'* passed under it. All these things are striking, and indicative of great good from the altered feeling of the country.

We reached the Tuileries at a few minutes before eleven, and got out for a few minutes to change to the State carriages, which, with escort-staff, &c., were waiting when we arrived. Everything seemed always most beautifully arranged, everything ready to the minute, never a moment's delay. Prince Napoleon met us there, and the dear Empress accompanied us downstairs, where we had to wait a little while till everyone had got into the carriages. The rooms below, leading to the great entrance, which you drive under, and which are under the Pavillon de Flore (I think), we had not been through yet. At length our carriage appeared; so I had to take leave of the dear Empress, which I did with great sorrow, as she is such a dear, sweet, engaging, and distinguished being, a fairylike *Erscheinung*, unlike anyone I ever saw. She was in tears, much grieved at parting, and at not being able to accompany us to the station. Most truly and sincerely do I wish her all possible happiness.

Vicky was melted in tears, *selon son habitude*; she is much devoted and attached to the Empress. We then entered the fine carriage (the usual closed State one) with eight splendidly harnessed horses, and one postilion in the old French style, with high boots and cocked hat, on the farthest horse, and grooms running by the side of the horses – six horses being *attelés* to, I think, three of the other carriages. We, with Vicky, went with the Emperor in this fine carriage.

The streets, windows, and houses were immensely crowded, and the people were more enthusiastic than ever. The enthusiasm seems to have gone on increasing. We went along the Rue de Castiglione, Rue de la Paix, Place Vendôme (where Napoleon's statue stands on that high column made out of Austrian cannon), the Boulevard St-Denis, and up the fine Boulevard de Strasbourg to the station. Alas! it was our last view of that gay, brilliant town, where we have been so kindly received, and for which I shall ever have an affectionate feeling.

At the station were all the ministers and *autorités*, of whom we took leave. I gave M. Fould a snuff-box, asking him into the *wagon* to wish him good-bye, and gave my hand to my favourite old Maréchal Vaillant.

Prince Napoleon got into the *wagon* with the Emperor, ourselves, and the children. The heat tremendous, both in the carriages and on the railroad, where the dust was quite dreadful. Prince Napoleon was more pleasant, which was fortunate, considering that we had him for five hours with us in the carriage.

I showed the Emperor a nice letter I had received from Ernest Leiningen,[1] giving an account of the attack on Sweaborg, and he showed me one he had received from a general. When we were in the carriage on Saturday, going to St-Germain, we showed the Emperor General Simpson's despatches, and the confidential report from Sir H. Jones[2] and General

1. Prince Ernest Leiningen, elder son of the Queen's half-brother Charles, Prince of Leiningen, and later an Admiral in the British Navy.
2. Lieut.-Gen. Sir Henry Jones, a member of Lord Raglan's staff in the Crimea.

MONDAY, AUGUST 27th

Niel[1], giving the numbers necessary for the trenches, and what the actual numbers there are, and the Emperor exclaimed with sorrow: '*Mon Dieu! voilà que je n'ai* 58,000 *baïonnettes!*'

We passed Pantin, Clermont (after which we had our luncheon, as on the day of our arrival, on two or three little tables which were brought in by the Emperor's valet, who was in the next carriage), Amiens, Abbeville, &c., but got out nowhere. Everywhere immense crowds and great enthusiasm. There was quite an *attroupement* of National Guards at Abbeville, who were anxious to get a good sight. At length, at half-past five, we arrived at the station at Boulogne. Here there was an immense crowd. The Maréchal Baraguay d'Hilliers, and several generals, &c., received us. The Emperor, Albert, and Prince Napoléon mounted their horses, the Emperor and Albert riding on either side of the carriage (everyone in uniform, and Bertie in his Highland dress). Vicky, Bertie, and Janie Ely were in the open carriage with me, driving *en poste*. It was a gay scene, and the evening beautiful.

We drove at once to the Hôtel du Pavillon, which is *sur la plage* and quite close by. We got out here for a moment *pour nous arranger un peu*, and then re-entered the carriage, and the Emperor and Albert, &c., mounted their horses. The *Cent-Gardes*, who travelled with us on the railroad, and always were on guard at every station which we stopped at, formed

1. General (later Maréchal) Adolphe Niel was responsible for establishing the Garde Mobile as a means of reinforcing the Army immediately before the Franco-Prussian War.

[145]

the escort. We drove down at once to the sands immediately below the hotel, where were assembled all the troops of the camp, 36,000 infantry, besides two regiments of cavalry, *Lanciers*, and *Dragons*, and the *Gendarmerie*. We drove down the lines, which were immensely deep, quite a forest of bayonets. The effect they produced with the back-ground of the calm blue sea, and the setting sun, which threw a glorious and crimson light upon it all, for it was six o'clock, was most magnificent. When this ceremony was over we took our places in order to see the marching past; but before that, the Emperor distributed some crosses of the *Légion d'honneur* to some officers and non-commissioned officers. This was an interesting sight. They were brought up in front of all the troops, those bearing the eagles standing foremost, and one by one these men came up to the Emperor (who was on horseback), and he fastened the cross on each man's breast, shaking hands with him afterwards. There were not enough decorations for all those who were to receive them. Accordingly, with these he only shook hands. The Maréchal said: *'S'ils ont la parole de Votre Majesté qu'ils l'auront, cela leur suffit.'*

There was an officer who, while we were driving in, the Maréchal expressed his wish to the Emperor, should be promoted, and the Emperor said he saw no particular reason, *'mais si la Reine le désire, je le ferai.'* He told me this, and I naturally said I should be too happy; and when this officer advanced to thank the Emperor, he sent him up to me to thank me, which was *très-gracieux de l'Empereur.*

This over, they began to *défiler*, which took a long time ... They walk much looser than our men, but they keep their time well, and their appearance and step are very soldierlike, and their clothes well made, and sitting so well. Their bands are very large, and their drums (brass ones) excellent. They came by, as usual crying: *'Vive la Reine d'Angleterre,' 'Vive l'Empereur, l'Impératrice,'* &c.

Near the end of the marching past our squadron saluted; and indeed it was one of the not least remarkable of the many striking events and contrasts with former times, which took place during this visit, that at this very place, on these very sands, Napoleon I reviewed his army, which was to invade England, Nelson's fleet lying, where our squadron lay, watching that very army. Now our squadron saluted Napoleon III while his army was filing past the Queen of England, several of the bands playing *Rule Britannia*. The two sovereigns, the one the nephew of the first Napoleon, the other the grand-daughter of George III, his bitterest foe, and these two sovereigns and the two nations bound together by the closest alliance which has almost ever existed between two great independent nations. May this ever continue so, and receive God's blessing!

The sight of the troops as they filed off in their separate battalions of 800 each along the seashore, the setting sun gilding the thousands of bayonets, lances, &c., was indescribably beautiful.

We then drove up towards the camp, which is on the heights, quite close to Honvault. Mme de Rayneval (unmarried) was in the carriage with me. We got out before we drove into the camp, to see some experiments made with new and very large *fusées incendiaires*, the Emperor's own invention which can go three miles, but the results were not entirely satisfactory. Re-entering the carriages, we drove up into the camp, which extends over a very large space. The huts are very low and small, ill-ventilated, made of mud, and with no *floors*. We got out to look into one of the men's and an officer's, and tasted some of their excellent brown bread.

The moon was now rising like a crimson ball, and giving a beautiful effect to the darkening sky and the dim twilight. I had a *cantinière* called up to the carriage, and looked at her dress and her little barrel. She was very tidy, clean, and well-spoken. I wish we had them in our army. They must always be married, and if they wish to remain in the regiment, and their husband dies or is killed, they must marry again within the year.

We got back to the hotel by eight, and at about twenty minutes past eight we dined. All the gentlemen and ladies attached to us, Lord and Lady Cowley, some of the Emperor's aides-de-camp, Maréchal Baraguay d'Hilliers, and three other generals, Sir Thomas Cochrane,[1] Baron J. Rothschild,[2] &c., were of the party. The two children also dined with us.

1. Admiral of the Fleet, Commander-in-Chief at Portsmouth.
2. Baron James Rothschild, the banker, who participated in important financial operations with the French government under both King Louis-Philippe and the Second Empire.

I sat between the Emperor (I was truly grieved to think for the *last* time) and Prince Napoleon. The Emperor was very cheerful, and made us laugh by talking of the concert last night, which he thought *'terriblement ennuyeux.'* Speaking of its being the last evening, which grieved me so and made me so sad, he said: *'Vous m'inviterez, n'est-ce pas, à Windsor, l'année prochaine?'* To which I replied I should be too happy. *'Et alors vous viendrez à Fontainebleau?'* I should be equally happy to do that, but he knew I was not so much mistress of my own actions as he was, which he would not admit in matters of this kind.

After dinner the company sat talking and making a great noise in a large room, at the end of which was a small one with two large folding doors, which were open, where we sat with the Emperor, Prince Napoleon, and the children, talking and looking at some of my photographs of the officers, &c., in the Crimea, which I had brought on purpose. This continued till near eleven, when we went upstairs to put on our shawls and bonnets. While I was doing this, the Emperor (who had expressed through Lord Cowley his great wish that Albert would accept it), gave Albert the small cross or rather medal, instituted by himself, and which is worn by the whole French army. It is a medal with the Emperor's head on it, surmounted by an eagle, and attached to a green and yellow ribbon. When I came in Albert said: *'L'Empereur a fait un bon soldat Français de moi.'* He took his own medal off and put it himself on Albert. He said to me: *'Je ne fais pas de si belles phrases que l'Empereur de Russie, mais elles sont plus sincères'*; which I am quite sure of, for it is that absence of *phrases* which is so pleasing in him, and which makes one value deeply any little expression, any kind look and observation, so much more.

We got into the carriages. The town, streets, and houses were one blaze of illuminations and fireworks. There were salutes, bands playing, great cheering, and, to crown all, an exquisite moon shining brilliantly over everything. It was a very fine and moving sight. The Emperor led me on board, followed by his whole suite, as he wished to go with us a little way out to sea. We glided out of the harbour – I with a heavy heart, having bid adieu to beautiful and most enjoyable France, where we have met with a reception we never can forget, and for which I shall ever retain a most affectionate feeling.

The salutes and fireworks were going on all round us, and all the ships showed blue lights. When out of the port we took the Emperor, who was in perfect amazement at the size of the yacht, all over it below; he wishes to build one smaller for himself. I said he should build one the same size, to which he replied: *'Cela va pour la Reine des Mers, mais pas pour un terrestrien comme moi.'* When we came on deck Colonel Fleury told the Emperor he must leave, or his small yacht, *l'Ariel*, could not re-enter the port.

We thanked the Emperor much for all his kindness and for this delightful visit. He said, *'Vous reviendrez?'* and we hoped he would come to England. I embraced him twice, and he shook hands very warmly with

Albert and the children. We followed him to the ladder, and here I once more squeezed his hand and embraced him, saying, *'Encore une fois, adieu, Sire!'* We looked over the side of the ship and watched them getting into the barge. The Emperor called out, *'Adieu, Madame; au revoir!'* to which I replied, *'Je l'èspere bien'*. We heard the splash of the oars and saw the barge, lit by the moon, and numbers of blue lights which we had on board the yacht, row up to the *Ariel*, and the Emperor and the rest go on board the yacht. Then we sent up endless rockets. We waited a little while for the *Fairy* to bring up the baggage, and watched the Imperial yacht, which passed us, and which our men cheered, while we waved our hand kerchiefs, and then *all* was still – all over ... It was past twelve when the Emperor left, and we stayed talking with Lord Clarendon, &c., till one.

Strange indeed are the dispensations and ways of Providence. Who ever could have thought that this same man, this Emperor, towards whom we certainly were not, since December, 1851, well disposed, against whom so much was said, whose life had been so chequered, could from outward circumstances and his own sincere, straightforward conduct towards this country, and moderation and wisdom generally, become not only the staunchest ally and friend of England, but our personal friend?

I have since frequently talked with Albert, who is naturally much calmer, and particularly much less taken by people, much less under *personal* influence than I am. He quite admits that it is extraordinary

how very much attached one becomes to him when
one lives with the Emperor, quite at one's ease and
intimately, as we have done during the last ten days,
for eight, ten, twelve, and to-day even fourteen hours,
a day. He is so quiet, so simple, naïf even, so pleased
to be informed about things which he does not know,
so gentle, so full of tact, dignity, and modesty, so full
of respect and kind attention towards us, never saying
a word or doing a thing which could put me out or
embarrass me. I know few people whom I felt – in-
voluntarily I may say – more inclined to confide in
and speak unreservedly to. I should not fear saying
anything to him. I felt – I do not know how to express
it – safe with him. His society is particularly agreeable and pleasant; there is something fascinating,
melancholy, and engaging, which draws you to him
in spite of any *prévention* you may have against him.
He certainly has a most extraordinary power of
attaching people to him! The children are very fond
of him; to them also his kindness was very great, but
at the same time most judicious. Then he is so fond
of Albert, appreciates him so thoroughly, and shows
him so much confidence. In fine, I shall always look
back not only on this visit to France, on account of the
delightful and splendid things we saw and enjoyed
there, but on the time we passed with the Emperor
as one of the pleasantest and most interesting periods
of my life. The Empress, too, has a great charm, and
we are all very fond of her.

We only got to bed at a quarter to two – I low,
bewildered, and excited.

I could hardly believe it when, at half-past eight, the yacht stopped, and we heard we were at Osborne. Incredible! Transported in one night from that gay brilliant scene! We took leave of Lord Clarendon, who enjoyed this visit greatly, Lord Abercorn, Mary Bulteel, and General Grey.[1] The others came on shore with us. We found Affie and the two little boys below on the beach, all looking extremely well; Affie and Arthur delighted to see us again. Near the house were Lenchen and Louise, and in the house poor dear Alice, who was quite upset at seeing us. Felt dreadfully bewildered, excited, and unable to do anything but think and talk all day of everything to Lady Caroline Barrington,[2] Skerret,[3] &c., and recalling every little incident, many of them very amusing.

Before I close the account of this ever memorable and delightful visit I will just add a few remarks about the principal Palaces, which ought to have been in their proper place, but which, from multitudinous interruptions, I omitted.

In the first place, as regards St-Cloud. It has taken its name from St Clodoald, grandson of Clovis, who

1. Lieut.-General the Hon. Charles Grey, Equerry and Private Secretary to Prince Albert.
2. Lady Superintendent to the Princesses.
3. Marianne Skerret, the Queen's principal dresser.

resided there as a hermit. Henriette d'Angleterre, Duchesse d'Orléans, died there. The Tuileries were so called from having been a tile-field in the time of Charles VI of France; Francis I bought it for his mother, Louise of Savoy. Then Catherine de Médicis built great part of it; Louis XIV lived only a short time there. In the three Revolutions of 1789, 1830 and 1848, the mob attacked it and went into it. The Louvre, begun by Henry II, continued by Francis I. They, as well as Charles IX, Henry III and Henry IV, who was brought there after he had been stabbed, and expired there (they showed me the staircase up which he had been carried), lived there and added to it. Louis XIV rebuilt a good deal of it; Napoleon carried it on; and now it is being finished by the present Napoleon. The Elysée was built for Mme de Pompadour. Napoleon lived there, as did the Murats, la Reine Hortense, and afterwards the Duc de Berri; the Duchesse of Parma (Mademoiselle) having been born there.

Versailles was an ancient hunting lodge, built by Louis XII. Louis XIV, when he left St Germain (the ancient palace of the kings, and where Charles IX and Louis XIV were born, and Louis XIII died), built this splendid palace, which was then added to by Louis XV (who built the theatre), by Louis XVI, and finally by Louis-Philippe. The theatre was first used in honour of Louis XVI's marriage, and then for the birth of the Dauphin his son. The Grand Trianon was built by Louis XIV for Mme de Maintenon; and the Petit Trianon, for Mme Du Barry, by Louis XV. On the Boulevard des Italiens, Albert and the Emperor pointed out to me the house from which Fieschi[1] fired his infernal machine.

I want also to make some mention of Maréchal Baraguay d'Hilliers. The Maréchal is a clever, but ill-tempered man, who seems to be on no good terms with Maréchal Vaillant, who calls him '*l'enfant gâté de l'Empereur*,' as the Emperor himself told me. He was a short time Ambassador at Constantinople, and quarrelled dreadfully with Lord Stratford. He commanded at Bomarsund, and lost his left hand at the battle of Leipzic. He is a fine-looking, tall man.

One ridiculous incident I wish also to add. The evening of our arrival, just as we were entering the Bois de Boulogne, the Emperor called to Marshal Magnan, and said: '*Dites à Lepicq*' (who commands the *Cent-Gardes*) '*d'aller avertir l'Impératrice que la Reine d'Angleterre arrive.*' After a few minutes, Colonel Lepicq comes up to the carriage, salutes, and says: '*Sire, le Maréchal Magnan fait annoncer à votre Majesté que la Reine d'Angleterre est arrivée.*' '*Comment! mais elle est ici,*' the Emperor exclaimed, and sent him off to the Empress; after which we all burst out laughing, and the Emperor said: '*Diable! c'est par trop fort,*' and laughed heartily.

1. A Corsican who, on July 28, 1835, made an attempt on the life of King Louis-Philippe.

Appendix

It has been agreed upon in consultation between the Emperor of the French and Her Majesty's Government, as follows:

1. Whether the result of the fire now opened upon Sebastopol be favourable or otherwise, that such measures shall be taken as, while they secure the siege materials from risk, shall not require a larger force than 60,000 men for holding the present position of the trenches, or for holding the town if it should have been taken.

2. That the rest of the allied forces be rendered available for field operations with a view to ensuring the complete investment of Sebastopol after the defeat or dispersion of the Russian field army.

3. That with this object they be further divided into two armies of operation.

4. That the investing army be composed of 60,000 men, of whom 30,000 shall be French and 30,000 Turks, under the command of General Canrobert.

5. That the first army of operation be composed of the British army (say) 25,000 men, and the Sardinian contingent of 15,000 men, and of 5,000 French troops, and

10,000 Turks if possible – in all not less certainly than 45,000 men, under the command of Lord Raglan.

6. That the second army of operation be composed of 45,000 French, now before Sebastopol, and 25,000 French, now assembling in reserve at Constantinople – in all 70,000 men, under the personal command of the Emperor, or such person as he may appoint.

7. That the plan of operations and mode of combining them be left for decision on the spot.

8. For the purpose of carrying on the above, it is understood, that orders are to be given to Generals Canrobert and Lord Raglan to take the necessary steps for rendering their troops available for the intended services; that all the troops of both countries are to be concentrated before Sebastopol as complete and as soon as possible, except the 25,000 French troops now concentrating at Constantinople; that the Sardinian contingent is to proceed at once to Balaclava; and that all the means of steam transport now in the Mediterranean and Black Sea after landing the Sardinian contingent and the French troops for whom vessels have been ordered to Marseilles, are to be left in the Black Sea.

(*Signed*)	(*Signed*)
Subscribed by command	*Par ordre de l'Empereur*
of Her Majesty	*Ml. Ministre de la Guerre*
PANMURE	VAILLANT

April 21st, 1855

Index

Abercorn, Marquis of, 77n., 153
Aberdeen, Lord, 15, 48; his Government, 14
Adalbert, Prince, 85, 88, 111, 113, 117, 125, 127, 139
Affie, see Alfred, Prince
Albany, Duke of, see Leopold, Prince
Albe, Duc d', 137; Duchesse de, 89, 103, 108, 111, 125, 137
Alfred, Prince, 36, 42, 153
Alice, Princess, 36, 42, 153
Amélie, Queen, see Marie-Amélie, Queen
Anglesey, Lady, 64
Argyll, Duchess of, see Louise, Princess
Arthur, Prince, 26, 28, 36, 40, 42, 52, 55, 58, 61, 153
Augusta of Prussia, Princess, 17
Augustenburg, Duke of, 127; Princess of, 125
Aumale, Duc d', 137

Bacciochi, Count, 95, 102, 118; Princesse, 102
Barrington, Lady Caroline, 153
Bassano, Duc de, 39, 46, 102; Duchesse de, 133
Beauharnais, Comte de, 85n.
Belgians, King of the, (uncle) 17, 35, 100n., 135n.; Queen of the, 131, 135n.
Belmont, M. le Comte de, 77, 99
Bertie, see Wales, Prince of
Biddulph, Colonel, 77n., 100
Bismarck, Count, 125
Bonaparte, Louis, 85n.
Boulogne, review at, 146–7
Breadalbane, Marquis of, 77n.
Brumaire, le 10, 88; Révolution du 18, 140
Bulteel, Hon. Mary, 77n, 101, 153, Burgoyne, Sir J., 41, 55

Cambacérès, Duc de, 102
Cambridge, Duchess of, 37, 38, 40, 42, 43, 44, 49, 62; Duke of, see George, Prince; Princess Mary of, 14, 37, 38, 39, 40, 43, 49, 62
Canning, Lady, 28
Canrobert, General, 82, 87, 114, 136, 156, 157
Cardigan, Lord, 37

Caroline, Princess, 102
Catte, Général de, 102
Champs-de-Mars (review), 113–15
Charles, see Leiningen, Prince Charles
Charles I (of England), 50
Charles VI, 154
Charles IX, 107, 154
Charles X, 140, 61, 107
Chartres, 135, see also Duke of Orléans
Christina, Queen, 123
Churchill, Lady, 77n.
Clarendon, Lady, 16
Clarendon, Lord, 13, 14, 15, 16, 17, 19, 20, 41, 59, 77n., 104, 118, 119, 151, 153
Clém, see Clémentine, Princesse
Clémentine, Princesse, 25
Cochrane, Sir Thomas, 148
Connaught, Duke of, see Arthur, Prince
Convention, the, 88, 109, 140
Cowley, Lady, 86, 100, 106–7, 111, 125, 148
Cowley, Lord, 18, 41, 70, 73, 86, 148, 149
Crimean War, 21, 33n., 38n., 41, 51n., 64n., 82n., 96, 105, 136; defects of generals, 117; Memorandum on the conduct of, 59, 156–7; opposition to Napoleon III visiting, 16, 47-8, 57, 61; origins of, 14; Russian losses in, 80, 83
Crystal Palace, see Great Exhibition

Dauphin, 104, 154

Ely, Lady (Jane), 29, 52, 68, 69, 77n., 100, 112, 118, 132, 145
Edinburgh, Duke of, see Alfred, Prince
Ernst of Saxe-Coburg-Gotha, Prince, 17
Essling, Princess d', 32, 36, 45, 77, 102, 112, 138
Eu, Château d', 18, 25, 114, 120n., 140; Forêt d', 120
Exposition des Beaux-Arts, 53, 84, 91, 97, 104, 113, 121, 132

Fleury, Colonel, 16, 46, 47, 77, 150
Fould, M. Achille, 78, 83, 84, 144

[158]

INDEX

François Ferdinand, *see* Joinville, Prince de

Gainsborough (Fanny), Duchess of, 126
George, *see* George, Prince
George III, 39, 116, 147
George, Prince, 15, 28, 31, 33, 37, 39, 40, 42, 44, 45, 49, 65, 66
Gloucester, (Aunt), Duchess of, 59
Grange, Marquis de la, 77
Great Exhibition, 50, 52, 56–8, 108
Grey, Lieut.-General the Hon. Charles, 77*n.*, 153

Hardinge, Lord, 41
Haussmann, Baron, 19, 63, 98, 110; *and* Madame, 110, 111
Helena, Princess, 36, 153
Henri II, 107, 154
Henri III, 140, 154
Henri IV, 106, 154
Henry VI, 18
Hesse, Grand Duchess of, *see* Alice, Princess
Hilliers, Maréchal Baraguay d', 73, 145, 146, 148, 155
Holland, Queen of, *see* Hortense, la Reine
Hortense, la Reine, 29*n.*, 85, 98, 109, 154
Hôtel de Ville, 63, 86, 99; ball at, 98, 106, 110

Invalides, Hôtel des, 115, 116, 117*n.*
Isabella II of Spain, 35, 123*n.*

Jérôme, cousin, *see* Napoleon, Prince Jérôme
Joinville, Prince de, 35, 137
Jones, Lieut.-General Sir Henry, 144
Joseph, le Roi, 62
Josephine, Empress, 46, 85*n.*, 98, 109, 122

Kent, Duchess of (Mama), 26*n.*, 28, 31, 33, 35, 44, 62, 65, 93
Kreuzzeitung, 125

Labédoyère, Madame, 77, 118, 126
Lablache, Luigi, 46, 120
Lansdowne, Lord, 12
Leiningen, Emich Charles, Prince of, 26*n.*
Leiningen, Prince Charles, 26, 28, 31, 33, 36, 40, 43, 44, 50, 51, 57, 67, 68, 144*n.*
Leiningen, Prince Ernest, 144
Lenchen, *see* Helena, Princess
Leopold I of Bavaria, 85*n.*
Leopold, Prince, 35
Leopold, uncle, *see* Belgians, King of the
Lhuys, M. Edouard Drouyn de, 64, 100, 103; *and* Madame, 100
Little Arthur, *see* Arthur, Prince
Louis XII, 154
Louis XIII, 154
Louis XIV, 90, 91, 92, 93, 122, 126, 140, 154
Louis XV, 90, 91, 93, 127, 154
Louis XVI, 50, 86, 91, 93, 100, 127, 154
Louis XVIII, 107, 117
Louis-Philippe, King, 13, 18, 25*n.*, 27, 35*n.*, 64, 84, 90, 91, 92, 98, 100, 103, 111, 120, 123, 131, 135, 137, 138, 148*n*, 154, 155*n*
Louise, Aunt, *see* Belgians, Queen of the
Louise, Princess, 36, 153
Lowestine, Général, 75, 78

Magnan, Maréchal, 75, 78, 120, 155
Maintenon, Madame de, 91, 92, 154
Malaret, Madame de, 32, 45
Mama, *see* Kent, Duchess of
Marie, *see* Würtemberg, Duchess Alexander of
Marie-Amélie, Queen, 25, 35, 130, 135, 136–7
Marie Antoinette, 15, 86, 91, 92, 93, 100, 104, 107, 109, 127
Massena, Marshal, 45
Mathilde, Princesse, 19, 77, 78, 88, 95, 102, 103, 104, 106, 110–11, 114, 115, 117, 125, 127, 136, 139
Monsieur, 140
Montebello, Comtesse de, 39, 45, 46, 133; *and* Général Comte de, 46
Montijo, Comtesse, 17, 88, 102, 111, 137

Naples, King of, *see* Joseph, le Roi
Napoleon I, 12, 14, 58*n.*, 62, 78, 85, 87, 89, 90, 91, 92, 98, 107, 115–117, 133, 140, 142, 144, 147, 154
Napoleon, Charles, 98

INDEX